China: Lessons from Practice

Wang Maorong, *Shanghai Second Institute of Education*
Lin Weihua, *Shanghai Second Institute of Education*
Sun Shilu, *National Education Science Leading Group*
Fang Jing, *Shanghai Adult Education Research Society*
Editors

NEW DIRECTIONS FOR CONTINUING EDUCATION
GORDON G. DARKENWALD, *Editor-in-Chief*
Rutgers University

ALAN B. KNOX, *Consulting Editor*
University of Wisconsin

Number 37, Spring 1988

Paperback sourcebooks in
The Jossey-Bass Higher Education Series

Jossey-Bass Inc., Publishers
San Francisco • London

Wang Maorong, Lin Weihua, Sun Shilu, Fang Jing (eds.).
China: Lessons from Practice.
New Directions for Continuing Education, no. 37.
San Francisco: Jossey-Bass, 1988.

New Directions for Continuing Education
Gordon G. Darkenwald, *Editor-in-Chief*
Alan B. Knox, *Consulting Editor*

Copyright © 1988 by Jossey-Bass Inc., Publishers
and
Jossey-Bass Limited

Copyright under International, Pan American, and Universal
Copyright Conventions. All rights reserved. No part of
this issue may be reproduced in any form—except for brief
quotation (not to exceed 500 words) in a review or professional
work—without permission in writing from the publishers.

New Directions for Continuing Education is published quarterly
by Jossey-Bass Inc., Publishers (publication number USPS 493-930).
Second-class postage paid at San Francisco, California, and at
additional mailing offices. POSTMASTER: Send address changes to
Jossey-Bass Inc., Publishers, 350 Sansome Street, San Francisco,
California 94104.

Editorial correspondence should be sent to the Editor-in-Chief,
Gordon G. Darkenwald, Graduate School of Education, Rutgers
University, 10 Seminary Place, New Brunswick, New Jersey 08903.

Library of Congress Catalog Card Number LC 85-644750

International Standard Serial Number ISSN 0195-2242

International Standard Book Number ISBN 1-55542-916-5

Cover art by WILLI BAUM

Manufactured in the United States of America

Ordering Information

The paperback sourcebooks listed below are published quarterly and can be ordered either by subscription or single copy.

Subscriptions cost $48.00 per year for institutions, agencies, and libraries. Individuals can subscribe at the special rate of $36.00 per year *if payment is by personal check.* (Note that the full rate of $48.00 applies if payment is by institutional check, even if the subscription is designated for an individual.) Standing orders are accepted.

Single copies are available at $11.95 when payment accompanies order. (California, New Jersey, New York, and Washington, D.C., residents please include appropriate sales tax.) For billed orders, cost per copy is $11.95 plus postage and handling.

Substantial discounts are offered to organizations and individuals wishing to purchase bulk quantities of Jossey-Bass sourcebooks. Please inquire.

Please note that these prices are for the academic year 1987-88 and are subject to change without notice. Also, some titles may be out of print and therefore not available for sale.

To ensure correct and prompt delivery, all orders must give either the *name of an individual* or an *official purchase order number.* Please submit your order as follows:

Subscriptions: specify series and year subscription is to begin.
Single Copies: specify sourcebook code (such as, CE1) and first two words of title.

Mail orders for United States and Possessions, Australia, New Zealand, Canada, Latin America, and Japan to:
    Jossey-Bass Inc., Publishers
    350 Sansome Street
    San Francisco, California 94104

Mail orders for all other parts of the world to:
    Jossey-Bass Limited
    28 Banner Street
    London EC1Y 8QE

New Directions for Continuing Education Series
Gordon G. Darkenwald, *Editor-in-Chief*
Alan B. Knox, *Consulting Editor*

CE1 *Enhancing Proficiencies of Continuing Educators,* Alan B. Knox
CE2 *Programming for Adults Facing Mid-Life Change,* Alan B. Knox
CE3 *Assessing the Impact of Continuing Education,* Alan B. Knox

CE4	*Attracting Able Instructors of Adults*, M. Alan Brown, Harlan G. Copeland
CE5	*Providing Continuing Education by Media and Technology*, Martin N. Chamberlain
CE6	*Teaching Adults Effectively*, Alan B. Knox
CE7	*Assessing Educational Needs of Adults*, Floyd C. Pennington
CE8	*Reaching Hard-to-Reach Adults*, Gordon G. Darkenwald, Gordon A. Larson
CE9	*Strengthening Internal Support for Continuing Education*, James C. Votruba
CE10	*Advising and Counseling Adult Learners*, Frank R. DiSilvestro
CE11	*Continuing Education for Community Leadership*, Harold W. Stubblefield
CE12	*Attracting External Funds for Continuing Education*, John H. Buskey
CE13	*Leadership Strategies for Meeting New Challenges*, Alan B. Knox
CE14	*Programs for Older Adults*, Morris A. Okun
CE15	*Linking Philosophy and Practice*, Sharan B. Merriam
CE16	*Creative Financing and Budgeting*, Travis Shipp
CE17	*Materials for Teaching Adults: Selection, Development, and Use*, John P. Wilson
CE18	*Strengthening Connections Between Education and Performance*, Stanley M. Grabowski
CE19	*Helping Adults Learn How to Learn*, Robert M. Smith
CE20	*Educational Outreach to Select Adult Populations*, Carol E. Kasworm
CE21	*Meeting Educational Needs of Young Adults*, Gordon G. Darkenwald, Alan B. Knox
CE22	*Designing and Implementing Effective Workshops*, Thomas J. Sork
CE23	*Realizing the Potential of Interorganizational Cooperation*, Hal Beder
CE24	*Evaluation for Program Improvement*, David Deshler
CE25	*Self-Directed Learning: From Theory to Practice*, Stephen Brookfield
CE26	*Involving Adults in the Educational Process*, Sandra H. Rosenblum
CE27	*Problems and Prospects in Continuing Professional Education*, Ronald M. Cervero, Craig L. Scanlan
CE28	*Improving Conference Design and Outcomes*, Paul J. Ilsley
CE29	*Personal Computers and the Adult Learner*, Barry Heermann
CE30	*Experiential and Simulation Techniques for Teaching Adults*, Linda H. Lewis
CE31	*Marketing Continuing Education*, Hal Beder
CE32	*Issues in Adult Career Counseling*, Juliet V. Miller, Mary Lynne Musgrove
CE33	*Responding to the Educational Needs of Today's Workplace*, Ivan Charner, Catherine A. Rolzinski
CE34	*Technologies for Learning Outside the Classroom*, John A. Niemi, Dennis D. Gooler
CE35	*Competitive Strategies for Continuing Education*, Clifford Baden
CE36	*Continuing Education in the Year 2000*, Ralph G. Brockett

Contents

Editors' Notes 1
Lin Yanzi, Phyllis Cunningham

1. The Social Context of Adult Education in China 5
Wang Maorong
The history of adult education both before and after the revolution of 1949 shows that adult education, its agencies, institutions, and administration is a response to the needs of the revolutionary struggle and socialist economic construction.

Part 1. Types of Adult Education

2. Literacy and Postliteracy Adult Education 15
Zhao Wenqing
Governmental policies, social forces, institutions, and peasant schools help to reduce greatly the illiteracy rate among the peasants. Adult education programs also are raising the peasants' levels of agricultural technology.

3. Rural Adult Education 23
Gu Genglin
TV universities, correspondence schools, polytechnical schools, and peasant middle schools are developing rapidly to meet the needs of rural economic changes.

4. Worker Education 33
Zeng Yiziang, Li Guohua, Wu Tiaogeng
Degree and nondegree programs in large, medium, and small enterprises are preparing specialists and improving workers' morale and skills to meet the needs of the four modernizations.

5. Cadre Education 45
Lin Jixiang, Zhou Maosheng
Policies, purposes, content, administration, and participants at the Shanghai Party School serve as examples of cadre education.

6. Adult Social Education 53
Zhu Yuancheng
Exhibitions, lectures, book reading and reviews, opera singing, stamp collecting, chess, and fishing are some of the social education programs offered by worker cultural palaces run by the trade unions.

7. Special Adult Education   59
Zhang Wanbing, Wang Xiaolai, Li Lei
Through programs initiated by the government, associations, and foundations, the physically and mentally handicapped are getting their education through formal colleges, TV, correspondence, and literacy classes.

Part 2. Types of Provision

8. Adult Institutional Provision   67
Fang Jing, Gao Zhuomin
There are over sixty adult higher education institutions in the City of Shanghai. Citizens can get their degrees, diplomas, and certificates from these and other institutions such as worker spare-time middle schools.

9. University Adult Provision   75
Lin Houxiang, Zhang Yi
Universities and colleges are running night colleges and correspondence programs for adults under forty years of age. Programs adapt to the characteristics of adult learners.

10. Postuniversity Provision   83
Zhou Qinggong, He Jie
Government, business and industrial sectors, academic associations and universities, as well as other social forces, provide supplementary, career change, and new technology programs through classes, lectures, academic exchanges, self study, TV, and correspondence to help engineers and researchers continue their education.

11. Distance Education   91
Gao Keming
Shanghai TV University has over three hundred full-time faculty and staff members who offer twenty-two academic majors in over two hundred courses. Distance education seeks to enhance cultural accomplishments and train qualified personnel for the whole nation.

12. Self-Study Adult Education   99
Cheng Bingyuan
Individuals can get their degrees through the regular state organized self-study examination system by completing required courses and passing the annual examinations.

Part 3. Professional Preparation and Research

13. Professional Preparation of Adult Educators 109
Jiang Keyi, Lin Weihua

Shanghai Second Institute, one of ten such adult educator training institutions, has ten departments to train teachers and administrators of adult provision, most of whom have not had formal training in adult education.

14. Research and Adult Education 117
Sun Shilu

Adult education associations, societies, and research institutes identify research topics, organize research projects, and disseminate findings through annual meetings, publications, and formal or informal exchanges.

Index 125

Editors' Notes

At the invitation of the International Task Force of the Commission of Professors of Adult Education, Lin Weihua, vice-president of the Shanghai Second Institute of Education (SSIE), and Sun Shilu, director of the Shanghai Adult Education Research Institute (SAERI), were sent in May 1986 by their respective groups to attend the North American Adult Education Research Conference. At the conference they presented an overview of adult education practice and research in China, and at that time it was suggested that a sourcebook on adult education in China published in the United States would be welcomed by North American adult educators and practitioners.

Shortly after Lin and Sun returned home, a meeting of the cadres was held, and it was decided that Wang Maorong, president of SSIE, would act as chief editor of the sourcebook, and Lin Weihua, Sun Shilu, and Fang Jing, deputy director of SAERI, would act as associate editors. Topics and content outlines were decided on, and specialists and practitioners familiar with adult education were invited to write the chapters. Lin Yanzi, a faculty member of SSIE and doctoral student at Northern Illinois University (NIU), and Phyllis Cunningham (NIU) were the English editors. Lin directed the team of translators (all graduate students at NIU), with editorial assistance from Chang Huifen (SSIE) and Vanessa Sheared (NIU); Becky Morey assisted with the typing.

The translators were Bao Xueming of East China Normal University (Chapters Eleven and Twelve); Lan Jiang of Zhenjiang Shipbuilding College (Chapter Five); Lan Shi of Shanghai Institute of Process Automation Instrumentation (Chapter Thirteen); Lin Yanzi of SSIE (Chapters One through Four, Nine, and Fourteen); and Tao Yu of SSIE (Chapters Six through Eight, and Ten).

Translators' Notes

A theorist in translation once said, "Translators are traitors." This is true in a sense. You can never translate a piece exactly and accurately without compromising understanding. So we translators must apologize to both the Chinese authors and the English readers for any inaccuracies or confusion. Owing to the differences in the two languages and cultures, it is difficult to translate the following terms, so an explanation of each is included.

1. *Worker education.* In Chinese this is called *chikong chiaoyu.* The term *chikong,* or *worker,* refers to all the members in an industrial

production entity, regardless of whether the person is a cadre, staff member, technician, specialist, engineer, or a laborer. Worker education might be best translated as "employee education." But the word *employee* has the connotation of employing, employed, and exploited. In China nobody employs anybody.

2. *Peasant education.* Peasants refers to a group of village farmers who farm nearby fields. In China today, however, *peasants* does not necessarily refer to those working only in the fields but includes people—village cadres, agricultural technicians, educated youth, and township enterprise workers (called "peasant workers")—who live and work in rural areas.

3. *Cadre education.* The word *cadre* has a wide range of meanings. Civil servants, teachers, doctors, engineers, professors, and officials are all cadres. But in this translation, the word *cadre* refers to those in the official governing, or leading, positions.

4. *Culture.* In the field of education, the Chinese word *culture* (*wenhua*) refers to one's education. So you can say that an illiterate has no culture and that a doctoral student has a very high culture. We have tried to avoid this word, using instead "educational level," "literacy," and "reading, writing, and calculation." But then there is the problem of translating the name of a "worker peasant culture school." You cannot translate it into a "worker peasant reading, writing, and calculating school." So we sometimes still use the word *culture* (that is, "culture education," "culture school," and "cultural and technical school").

5. *Talented people.* Mao Zedong once said to Deng Xiaoping, "You are a talented person." Deng is talented enough, but not all talented people, whom the Chinese education system is trying to prepare, are talented. "Talented people" in China refers to those who are capable of doing things that the common people cannot. A smart peasant can be called a talented person as can a university graduate. In translating this term, we try to use "specialist" and "qualified personnel" instead of "talented people." But the question is: "qualified" in and for what? So sometimes we must use the term. The reader should be aware that not everyone who is trained is "talented."

To aid the reader in understanding the Chinese adult education system, we have included a diagram of the system (see Figure 1).

Overview of Contents

Wang Maorong in Chapter One presents an introduction to the social context of adult education in China. The book then is divided into three major parts. In Part One, six types of adult education, as defined by specific populations, are described: literacy and postliteracy, rural, worker, cadre, social, and special. The authors of Chapters Two through Seven describe and illustrate the practice of adult education as it applies to these special populations.

Figure 1. China's Adult Education System

Level	Programs	
Higher Education	Four- to six-year degree programs offered by universities and colleges, correspondence, TV and broadcast, self-study examination system, and so on. Participants get university-based equivalent diplomas. Two- to three-year degree programs offered by the above-mentioned institutions or programs.	Short courses Single courses Single subjects Technical training Seminars Workshops Programs offered by party schools
Higher Secondary	Programs offered by technical schools, correspondence, TV and broadcast, general high schools, spare-time high schools, self-study examination system, and party schools.	
Lower Secondary	Programs offered by vocational schools, culture schools, cultural and technical schools, general secondary schools, spare-time schools, and party schools.	
Elementary	Literacy, literacy classes, programs offered by elementary or middle schools.	

Part 2 addresses the types of provision, including adult institutional, university, continuing professional (postuniversity), distance, and self-study education. The authors of Chapters Eight through Twelve describe policies and processes in detail.

Part 3 explores the professional preparation of adult educators and presents an overview of research activity in China; these final Chapters—Chapters Thirteen and Fourteen—complete the book.

Please note that most numerical data are obtained from local unpublished census figures. Accordingly, the reader will not always find references regarding sources in this volume. We trust that readers will learn as much as we have from reading about the practice of adult education in China and that the information gained will inform our practice of education.

Lin Yanzi
Phyllis Cunningham
English Editors

Lin Yanzi is a faculty member of the Shanghai Second Institute of Education and a doctoral student at Northern Illinois University.

Phyllis Cunningham is professor of leadership and educational policy studies at Northern Illinois University.

China has entered a new era in which economic construction has become a focus of the country; thus, many talented individuals are needed.

The Social Context of Adult Education in China

Wang Maorong

History of Adult Education in China

After the Opium War in 1948, China gradually turned into a semifeudal, semicolonial country. With the inception of the Old Democratic Revolution, revolutionaries such as Cai Yuanpei and Zhang Taiyian founded in 1902 a Chinese Education Society in Shanghai. These pioneers not only established general learning stations for adult remedial education but also opened up patriotic societies to disseminate revolutionary ideas and advocate equality between men and women. In 1912, when the Nanjing provisional government was established by Sun Yat-sen, Cai Yuanpei was appointed as minister of the Education Department. Cai, whose scholarly name is Renzi, established a Social Education Office within the department to promote adult education and mass social education. In the same year, the Renzi Outline was developed for remedial and vocational education. During World War I, China's national industry underwent expansion, creating a demand for basic adult and technical education. In response to this, the Chinese Vocational Education Society was founded in 1917. However, adult education in Old China could not center on industrial technology, since the industrial sector was too weak. Adult education could only develop in line with the democratic revolutionary movement.

The May Fourth Movement of 1919 was the turning point of the Old Democratic Revolution in China, which then became the New Democratic Revolution. Since the New Democratic Revolution began with a new cultural revolution, common people's education began to develop. Along with the student, peasant, and worker movement, various schools such as citizen, volunteer, worker, and peasant schools came into being. Among the famous schools were the Worker Night School of Changsha of the First Normal School of Hunan, established by Mao Zedong in 1917; the Changxin Dian Remedial School, sponsored by the People's Education Seminar of Beijing University, which was founded by Deng Zhengxia in 1919; and the Huxi Xiaoshado Worker School, opened by the Shanghai Communist Group in 1920. The purposes of these schools were to disseminate Marxist theory while teaching people to read and write. The goal was to impart rudimentary revolutionary ideas and encourage the laboring people to join the revolutionary struggle. Also during this period, a study-work movement was conducted in France by revolutionary pioneers such as Chou Enlai. This movement prepared some outstanding leaders and talented persons for the Chinese revolution.

Under the leadership of the Chinese Communist Party, which was founded in Shanghai in 1921, new cadre institutions such as the Hunan Self-Study University, the Shanghai University, the Peasant Movement Class, and the Shengang Labor College were opened. These institutions developed a great number of leaders for the First Revolutionary Civil War.

During the Second Revolutionary Civil War and the Anti-Japanese War, literacy education in the revolutionary bases began to develop as did cadre education. Institutions such as the Anti-Japanese Military and Political University, the North Shanxi College, and the Luxun Arts Academy prepared approximately twenty thousand cadres. Without these leading forces, the victory of the Anti-Japanese War and the birth of New China would not have been possible. After the founding of the New China in 1949, spare-time basic education programs were opened for cadres all over the country.

By 1949 modern Chinese adult education had begun, and developed in conjunction with the democratic revolution.

Achievements of China's Adult Education

The development of China's adult education after the democratic revolution can be divided into the following three periods:

1. *The developing period.* This period covers the years from 1949 to 1966. Great achievements were accomplished during these seventeen years: The illiteracy rate dropped from 80 to 43 percent; approximately 3 million illiterates were educated; and over 10 million individuals graduated from elementary, secondary, and higher education institutions.

2. *The stagnating period.* During the Ten Year Chaos (also known as the Great Cultural Revolution) from 1966 to 1976, adult education, like other educational enterprises, came to a standstill.

3. *The Redevelopment period.* After the Third Plenary Session of the Eleventh Conference of the Chinese Communist Party (December 18-22, 1978), especially during the period of the Sixth Five-Year Plan, adult education in China entered a new period. China's adult education has made great leaps forward in the scale of schools, the clientele served, and the quality of programs. Presently, there are more than 1,200 adult higher education institutions, over 4,000 secondary technical schools, 300,000 staff-worker schools, and 3,500 county-run peasant technical schools. There are 900,000 university and two-year college adult graduates and 1.4 million secondary technical school adult graduates. Furthermore, the illiteracy of over 1.5 million persons has been eliminated.

How is it that adult education has developed so rapidly within only eight or nine years?

First, China has entered a new era in which economic construction has become the focus of the country, and thus a great variety of talented individuals are needed. This need cannot be met by the regular educational institutions; therefore, adult education has the responsibility to train more talented people.

Second, reformation and the opening of China to the world requires that adult educators assist its people through educating and disseminating information on evolving trends and technical developments in other parts of the world. People have begun to realize that new information, techniques, and methods are necessary for functioning well in a highly skilled and technological society.

Needs become motivators that impel people to learn. The following examples illustrate these growing needs and the response of adult educators in China: (1) Since law and regulations are being stressed, law school education is needed; (2) to interpret these rules, the change in management of enterprises from governmental to economical methodology requires the study of economics; (3) the reliance of rural economic development on scientific farming, trading, and management of the township industry requires the study of innovative scientific techniques and technological advances.

Third, the policy that cadres must be revolutionary, informed, and specialized encourages cadres at all levels to actively participate in learning scientific techniques and technological skills.

Finally, the development of China's education relies on 400,000 indispensable teachers and staff. There are 200,000 administrators and 200,000 teachers in enterprises governed by the National Economy Committee. The great efforts demonstrated by these educators and practitioners have helped promote the rapid development of adult education in China.

Status and Functions of Adult Education in China

Although much has been gained, recognition of the status of adult education remains an issue in China because of traditional views about education and the fact that education is regarded as only marginally important by those in the labor force. The labor force has not realized that a great number of people do not have enough basic education or vocational training, nor do they realize that technical skills and expertise of workers are underdeveloped. The training of these workers is the responsibility of specialists, whose number is insufficient and whose knowledge and expertise are becoming obsolete. The professional training required in personnel management is also lacking. Therefore, it is impossible for the modern organizational management labor force to greatly increase production. Many fail to recognize that the level of political awareness, educational advancement, and technical quality within the labor force must be raised and that this cannot be achieved solely through the regular educational system.

Fortunately, things are changing. More and more people are beginning to see that if China wants to raise its moral and material levels, adult education is the main avenue. The National Adult Education Conference convened in Yantai, Shandong Province, in September 1986, pointed out that adult education is a very important part of China's educational enterprise.

China's whole educational enterprise can be divided into four categories: basic, technical, general higher education, and adult education. The first three types of education prepare future builders for the society and affect the future quality of the nation. Adult education serves those already working and can help raise the quality of the existing labor force directly; thus, it has an immediate effect on the economy and social services. This function alone justifies the importance of adult education. Adult education is recognized by most educators as a part of the national education. It is an enterprise that directly serves the social economy, influences the development of science and technology, and cannot be replaced by any other form of education.

The functions of adult education are many, but the following five functions are obvious and recognized: (1) inservice training, the purpose of which is to raise individuals' productive abilities; (2) completion of basic education; (3) adult higher education and secondary technical education (also referred to as degree education); (4) continuing education in which new knowledge and skills are acquired and disseminated; and (5) social cultural and life education, including the education of the elderly. These functions are not mutually exclusive, and, at any one time, one or two of these functions may become the focus. At present, inservice training is emphasized, but this does not mean that other functions are unimportant. Most adult educators define the functions of adult education in the above way, which shows that the function of adult education is commonly understood. The nature of adult education has been settled, and adult educational theory has developed into a new stage, providing a theoretical base for the status and importance of adult education.

The characteristics of adult education in China are derived from its functions. Adult educators in China hold different opinions as to what are the characteristics of China's adult education. We hold that there are basically two characteristics: The clientele, no matter what walks of life they represent, are working people. Most, therefore, need learning related to work. The second characteristic is of China's adult education spare-time learning.

Guidelines of China's Adult Education

At present, the general policy is that adult education should be developed and reformed to meet the needs of social development. Practices that violate the nature of adult learning must be reformed and conditions suitable to adult learning established.

Under the general policy, the following guidelines for adult education are being stressed:

1. *Development of job-related competence.* From this guideline it follows that learning is combined with practice, is based on needs, and is based on what people are doing in their jobs.

Under this guideline, the relationship between degree study and inservice training must be dealt with wisely. While we do not deny the importance of degree study, we do emphasize the training of the vast majority of workers, peasants, and cadres. Their training will increase their competence and quality and thus produce economic and social benefit.

The training should include a variety of forms, especially the problem-solving forms manifested in training classes as well as workshops and seminars for updating knowledge. Degree study should also be related to what the participants are doing and should stress the development of creative ability as well as application. The pursuit of a degree for the degree's sake is not encouraged.

In rural areas, the training of peasants and workers in township enterprises should stress practical techniques, and training of educated youth living in rural areas should be considered important. All resources including primary, secondary, and vocational school personnel; agricultural technicians; managers; specialized household members; and anyone who is competent should be mobilized to contribute to the training.

2. *Provision by institutions and organizations of adult educational service.* These bodies include governmental institutions, economic orga-

nizations and units, enterprises, universities, research institutes, democratic political parties, social agencies, and societies and associations. The efforts of party-free professionals should be recognized. The quality of adult education programs is regarded as important, regardless of who provides them.

3. *Provision of a variety of learning activities.* These learning activities include long- and short-term experiences, independent spare-time learning, and off-job and semi-off-job study and should be maintained and developed.

4. *Strengthening of the leadership and division of responsibilities at the central governmental level.* This is the responsibility of the State Commission of Education, which is also responsible for policy making, coordination, and adjustment. The commission controls the quality of degree study and accredits higher educational institutions. Other central departments are responsible for the direction of the vocational work in their respective adult education programs. Adult education programs in different subject matter areas are administered by leading bodies in their respective areas. This administration provides general direction and facilitates learning conditions but is not responsible for daily operations. The administration should be decentralized, that is, provinces, large cities, and autonomous regions should gradually shoulder the task so that local leadership and resources will be mobilized to better run adult education programs.

China's Adult Education and Lifelong Education

In China the concept that one should receive education throughout one's life is not new. Confucius, the ancient educator, knew this. He pointed out the moral, intelligence, and academic levels that one should reach in different periods of life, saying, "I was determined to learn when I was seventeen years old. At thirty I stood on my own feet. At forty, I dealt with things with full self-confidence. At fifty, I knew the heavenly mandate. At sixty, I became wise and shrewd. At seventy, I know whatever I should and can do whatever I want" (Soothill, 1968, p. 149). In order to reach these levels, one should always learn, pursue new knowledge, adapt to social development, and meet the needs of personal growth. The maxims are, as Confucius said, "Tireless in learning" and "Learning combined with practice." "The pursuit of knowledge is an endless effort" is a Chinese proverb passed on from generation to generation. Confucius is regarded by some educators as "the great oriental forerunner in lifelong education."

The idea that school education is limited and only one part of life while adulthood provides a more complex, comprehensive education was the concept on which famous rural educator, Lu Shiying, based his educational program over a half century ago.

Lifelong education focuses on the whole development of the individual. The life cycle is regarded as unified. The development of a human being is considered in conjunction with social life, economics, politics, and culture. Lifelong education is a theoretical system that stresses that education should be provided longitudinally (through one's whole life) and horizontally (taking into account societal factors).

From the very beginning, lifelong education has been implicit in China's education system. China has always stressed the connection of preschool education, middle and higher education, and adult education and has always advocated the combination of school, family, and social education. Adult continuing education and the education of the elderly have gained more emphasis recently, and great numbers of continuing education colleges have been opened. The administrative systems of science, technology, and education also take lifelong education into consideration.

Adult education in China is socialist adult education with typical Chinese characteristics. The purposes and objectives are to raise the quality of life for millions of laboring people; train and prepare thousands of specialists, administrators, and managers; and develop new types of talented people who are dedicated, moral, disciplined, and well informed so that eventually a powerful socialist new China can be built. As a part of the educational effort, adult education has a vast audience and will surely grow to maturity in the near future. Adult education is a beautiful flower in the educational garden, budding now and blooming soon.

Reference

Soothill, W. E. *The Analects of Confucius.* (2nd ed.) New York: Paragon, 1968.

Wang Maorong is president of Shanghai Second Institute of Education and a member of the Standing Committee of the Chinese Worker Education Research Society.

Part 1.

Types of Adult Education

When New China was founded in 1949, 80 percent of the population was illiterate. The peak of the literacy campaign was 1958 when 60 million were enrolled, following which the illiteracy rate dropped to 43 percent.

Literacy and Postliteracy Adult Education

Zhao Wenqing

Background

Since the founding of the People's Republic of China, literacy and peasant education has been developing rapidly. In 1949, 165 million illiterate young and middle-aged peasants comprised 80 percent of the peasant population. The central government recognized that eliminating illiteracy was an arduous task and immediately called on the nation to participate in this undertaking. Decrees such as The Decision on Literacy and The Directives for Literacy were promulgated. The commitment to literacy was written into the Constitution of China. The Decision on Literacy stipulated that a literacy campaign should be launched actively by the whole country in a well-planned way to help the people become literate. The standard of literacy was also defined in the decision: 2000 Chinese characters were to be mastered by a worker and 1,500 by a peasant. To become literate, one should have the ability to read ordinary books and newspapers, keep accounts, write simple notes, and do simple calculations with an abacus. The Directives for Literacy stipulates that illiteracy between the ages of twelve and forty-five should be "wiped out." That is to say, 85 percent of this age group should be made literate. The principles for literacy, as the directives say, are three: "Block out, wipe out, and raise up."

"Block out" means to stop the formation of new illiterates by instituting compulsory elementary education. Various means are adopted to guarantee that all children of school age go to school regularly and graduate with the required knowledge. "Wipe out" refers to the campaign to make most of the illiterates between the ages of twelve and forty-five literate. "Raise up" implies that new literates should be organized to participate in learning activities to maintain and raise their newly acquired knowledge levels.

Stimulated by the policies and organized by government at all levels, workers and peasants have plunged into the campaign, desiring to become masters of knowledge. The peak of this campaign was in 1958, when 60 million people were in literacy programs and a large number of people became literate.

According to the 1959 statistics, of 200 million young and middle-aged peasants, only 86 million were illiterate. The illiteracy percentage dropped from 80 percent in 1949 to 43 percent in 1959. Among illiterates, 40 percent could read more than 500 characters and 35 percent less than 500. The rest could not read any characters or were physically unable to learn.

The Cultural Revolution, and the ensuing Ten Year Chaos, acted as a setback to education. New illiterates emerged, and some literates became illiterates. In 1979 among the rural population aged 12 to 45, 120 million, or 30 percent, were illiterate. Most of these illiterates were either discovered during the revolution or were those who had just begun to learn the characters.

In 1979 the literacy movement was restored, and peasant education was established on a new basis. Peasant education administrative offices were set up or reestablished in most of the counties, cities, and prefectures, in all the provinces, and in centrally governed cities and autonomous regions. Full-time staff at the county and township levels numbered 54,000. Some teaching research units with full-time researchers were organized. Leadership was maintained at all levels.

All walks of life have been mobilized to fight illiteracy since then. In the period of the Sixth Five-Year Economic Development Plan (1980-85), the illiteracy of 15.2 million people was "wiped out" in the rural area. Presently, of the young and middle-aged rural population, only 18 percent are illiterate. Fifty percent of the population has reached the level of elementary education, and 30 percent is above the level of middle school. According to 1985 statistics, 1,400 counties almost wiped out illiteracy. However, in other areas the task of eliminating illiteracy is still difficult.

Peasant education is developing rapidly. At present, there are over 3,500 peasant technical schools at the county level, and 2,300 counties and villages have agricultural broadcasting schools. According to statistics from 15 provinces and cities, there are 17,000 peasant libraries, technical schools, and adult education centers. In 18 provinces, cities, and autonomous regions, 50 percent of the villages are running their own adult schools. In 1985 there were 25.3 million peasants participating in technical learning, making up 55 percent of all the registered peasant participants. This figure is ten times greater than that of 1980. This development is the result of the new structure of production and has greatly benefited the peasants.

Jilin Province's Literacy Program

The best way to understand how China conducts its literacy education among peasants is to examine one province, in this case, Jilin Province. Jilin province possesses all the characteristics of north China. The rural population is 14.9 million, which accounts for 66 percent of the province's population. The target population of peasant education is 5 million. When New China was founded, 90 percent of the rural population in this province was illiterate. Directed by the decisions and instructions from the central government, the province launched a great campaign to attack illiteracy. Ten years later, in 1958, 2.3 million individuals had become literate, and only 840,000 were still illiterate. The Ten Year Chaos halted the campaign, and illiteracy became a serious problem again.

The illiteracy rate amounted to 1.3 million in 1979 when the campaign was restored. From 1979 to 1982, 26,560 peasant night schools, 15,800 neighborhood literacy groups, and 125,846 one-to-one guaranteed teaching and learning groups were established. Altogether, the participants numbered 1.2 million. Postliteracy education also developed and grew, and more than 2 million adults participated in learning activities at the elementary and secondary levels. At the end of 1982, illiteracy and semi-illiteracy for 1.1 million people was eliminated, and the literacy rate for young and middle-aged peasants was over 96 percent. According to the standard set by the central government, the province has finished the historical mission of "wiping out" illiteracy. The International Literacy Award Committee of the United Nations conferred the province the Norma Award.

Plans, Rules, and Regulations of Literacy. Plans were based on a large survey of the whole province. The township government registered all village illiterates for age, sex, economic status, and former educational level. The target individuals were asked to participate in literacy programs and were encouraged to take off their "caps of illiteracy" within a certain period. Two plans were jointly considered and developed: (1) the literacy plan and (2) making elementary education universal.

To guarantee literacy education, the provincial government developed its own plan. The main points of the plan were the following:

1. A time limit of being literate was set based on individual situations.

2. Counties, cities, townships, small towns, and villages were to finish their literacy tasks in 1980 and 1982, and rules were to be developed by the prefectures (an administrative body consisting of a group of counties) and counties to encourage participation. For example, an illiterate should be taxed for literacy programs if he or she did not participate. The wedding registration of young illiterates was postponed. Recruitment of new workers was conducted through examinations. Young illiterate peasants were not employed by factories. Those who did not participate in learning were not nominated as model workers. Organizations not running a good literacy program did not become model organizations.

3. At the county and township levels, awards were organized to encourage model literacy workers, model teachers and participants, and model organizations. In 1982, when the province finished its literacy task, a provincial conference was held to present awards to 176 model organizations and 420 model individuals.

4. Worker-peasant education committees were formed at the government, township, county, prefecture, and province levels. Also established were relevant administrative offices within the general education system at all levels. Every township had its own full-time literacy staff. Thirty-six hundred officials, including those in charge of the task, were involved in the literacy program and formed a strong system of leadership.

Quality Control. Large-scale investigations were conducted each year to determine if the literacy movement was meeting the standards set by the central government. Official "literate certificates" were issued only to those who could recognize 1,500 characters, read short articles, and write simple, practical notices. Villages were the basic units evaluated to see if the literacy task was finished. Once literates comprised 85 percent of the population, a village was issued a Basically Nonilliterate Unit Certificate by the government.

Carrying Out the Block Out, Wipe Out, and Raise Up Principle. The province put great emphasis on universal elementary education. Elementary schools were asked to operate morning, noon, evening, and holiday or vacation classes to guarantee illiterates and semi-illiterates under the age of 15 the opportunity to study. Some illiterates were also allowed to "enroll" in regular classes. In this way 160,000 illiterates of this category became literate. At present, 98 percent of the school-age children attend school, and 97 percent stay at school regularly.

Flexibility and Practicality of Instruction. The target population of literacy was quite different in terms of age, working and living conditions, and learning styles. A variety of measures were adopted to address these special situations and conditions.

Forms and Organizations. For young illiterates, elementary schools assumed responsibility for organizing morning, noon, or evening classes or for letting these illiterates join a regular class in the middle of the course. In large villages, special literacy classes were opened for illiterates. Where middle and high schools existed, literacy classes were offered. For rural housewives who had many household chores, teachers went to the home and the teaching of characters was related to practical matters. Neighborhood learning groups and one-to-one guaranteed teaching and learning groups were also organized to suit conditions. In Jou Jiao Township of Jou Jiao County, 1,300 women were organized in 285 neighborhood groups and one-to-one teaching and learning groups. The result of such groups was that 1,250, or 90 percent, of the women became literate within a year.

Flexible Schedules. The schedule of the learning activities took into consideration the peasants' production schedule. "Learning more in slack seasons, learning less in farming seasons, and self-learning in busy seasons" was the principle governing the schedule. The "golden season" for literacy activities was the long winter, when full half-day classes could be run. During the farming seasons, evening classes were opened. During the busy season, independent learning activities were organized, with examinations at regular times to check the progress of the students.

Textbooks. Various textbooks were compiled to address the principle of meeting various needs in teaching. Literacy was combined with the dissemination of popular science and technology, including planting, animal husbandry, sewing, cooking, hygiene, machinery, and electronics. Counties, prefectures, and provinces compiled more than 1 million copies of 20 different literacy textbooks and reading material, including *Literacy Textbook with Phonetic Notation* and *Agricultural Technique Textbook*. Local areas also had their own teaching materials. Rural cultural palaces and libraries provided reading material for peasants.

Mobilization of the Populace. Literacy is an extensive mass activity involving millions of participants, an enormous number of teachers, and funds. The government relies on the population to solve the problems of teachers, space, and funds.

"Little Teachers." Under the principle of "Individual teaching individual, the able being the teacher," a contingent of over 60,000 part-time teachers was organized, and 300,000 elementary and middle school students were mobilized to act as "little teachers." These little teachers volunteered to teach after school and during vacations.

The whole province had 2,200 full-time literacy workers who organized teachers, made promotions, encouraged illiterates to participate, and assisted in teaching activities. Literacy teachers considered it a great honor to help the peasants, and model teachers emerged in every township.

Space and Funds. Any space, such as school classrooms, rural public buildings, or private homes, was used as teaching space. Funds were received from the local government, collective enterprises, peasant contributions, and profits pooled from work-study programs. Since 1979 the amount of funds has totaled 185 million yuan (Chinese dollars).

Postliteracy Peasant Education

Literacy is only the first step in the development of peasant education. Simple reading, writing, and calculating abilities cannot meet the needs of the four modernizations. Furthermore, resumption of illiteracy among new literates might occur unless postliteracy education is provided. Even elementary school graduates will return to a state of illiteracy or semi-illiteracy without follow-up learning. Examples can be found in the Qiangang and Chaigang townships. The former greatly emphasizes postliteracy education, and only 5 percent of new literates fall back into illiteracy. The latter neglects postliteracy education, and 16 percent lose their newly gained skills. Literacy and postliteracy are but two stages of peasant education. Literacy lays a solid foundation for postliteracy education, while postliteracy education consolidates and develops the achievement of literacy.

Under the new policy in China of dividing productive responsibilities among individuals, peasants have realized that science and technology are needed if production is to increase substantially. Peasants therefore want to learn more, and many are even willing to invest their own funds in intellectual development. This situation makes postliteracy peasant education a necessity.

In Jilin Province, for example, postliteracy education is in full operation. Eighty-seven percent of the villages have established sparetime elementary schools, enrolling 190,000 students. Over 4,000 secondary peasant vocational schools with 277,000 participants have been established and run by townships and villages. There are 1,162 branch schools of the Central Agricultural Broadcasting School, with 25,762 participants. At the county level, there are 10 peasant secondary technical schools and 4 two-year peasant technical colleges, with 3,200 students. Many workshops and seminars are conducted at these schools. A peasant educational system from elementary education to higher education has been established, and 2 million peasants are engaged in various learning activities in schools and classes.

Peasant Education: Present and Future

After several decades, peasant education in China has developed its own educational system, which consists of literacy; reading, writing, and technical education; secondary technical education; and higher technical education. Literacy attainment is the elementary stage in peasant education, though it also provides technical education. Since the task of literacy is almost completed and there is a change in the structure of peasant knowledge, literacy training will most likely disappear from the system of peasant education.

The main part of peasant education now is vocational education. At present vocational education has three functions: (1) to consolidate literacy advances; (2) to raise peasants' educational levels; and (3) to disseminate productive experience, knowledge, and techniques. Currently, peasant education emphasizes secondary technical skills along with the development of universal education. Peasant education in the future will focus on vocational education.

How to conduct peasant education more properly continues to be an issue. The fourth technological revolution will surely have an influence on peasant education. A new peasant generation is emerging. In addition to farming, many peasants now engage in trade, commerce, and management. In planning future programs of peasant education, the following guidelines should be stressed:

1. The requirements and form of education should take into consideration the needs and potentialities of peasants.

2. Peasant education should properly handle the relationship of seasonal technical training and the systematic study of science and technology.

3. Knowledge of scientific farming and fundamental production management should be stressed.

4. The needs of talented productive individuals at the local community level, as well as those in agriculture, industry, and trade, should be balanced and addressed.

5. Spare-time informal adult education programs should be given appropriate attention.

Summary

Literacy and postliteracy education have laid and reinforced a solid foundation for peasant education. Through literacy education programs, teachers and cadres are trained and developed, and the basis of cultural activities is established. The movement has provided valuable experiences ideologically, organizationally, and physically for the new development of peasant education in China.

Zhao Wenqing is director of the Adult Education Research Institute of the Education Committee of Jilin Province, China.

Through practice, peasants have begun to recognize the truth about science and technology: It is a means to help them to become rich.

Rural Adult Education

Gu Genglin

Changes in Economic Development

Since 1978 rural economic development has undergone a series of changes. These changes are due to the policies adopted at the Third Plenary Session of the Eleventh Conference of the Chinese Communist Party. The introduction of the "household contract," which allows individual entrepreneurship, and the adjustment of the rural economic structure helped impel the rural economy toward specialization, commercialization, and modernization. Self-sufficient production is turning into a commercial venture.

Structural Changes. The first change in rural economic reformation was the work point system. Productive responsibilities are now divided mainly through production contracts. This policy links peasants' pay directly to their productive output.

The second change was in the adjustment of the economic structure from a self-sufficient or semi-self-sufficient economy to a modern economy. Traditional agriculture is becoming commercialized. The specialized household is also a result of this change. Production is based on an individual family that specializes in producing certain commodities. The state-controlled market economy replaces the system of buying and selling only through the state, which challenges the peasant to become a "commercial peasant."

The Shift of the Labor Force. The development of commercial production in rural areas shifts the labor force from agriculture into the trades and industry. In 1985 approximately 76 million peasants, or 20 percent of the rural labor force, were engaged in rural trades and industry. It is estimated that one-third of all the peasants in China will engage in nonagricultural production in the next 20 years. This has already occurred in some of the more affluent areas in China. For example, in the Shanghai suburban districts, 70 percent of total revenues come from trades and industry, while agricultural productive value accounts for 15 percent. Only a small number of peasants still work in the fields. The peasants that have shifted to nonagricultural production desperately need to acquire knowledge of scientific methodology and techniques.

Science and Technology: The Key to Becoming Rich. Peasants have begun to realize that science and technology can help them become rich.

An article published in the *Peoples Daily*, March 22, 1983, reported the result of a survey conducted in Sheyang County of Jiangsu Province on the income of 194 peasant families. Seventeen percent of those with secondary educations had higher incomes than those with elementary educations, and incomes were twice as high compared to uneducated families.

The division of productive responsibilities has given peasants with better educations more access to scientific technology and methodology. The better-educated peasant also receives more information on means other than agriculture to increase income.

The first change in rural reformation motivated peasants to learn techniques that would raise production. The second change helped peasants acquire other knowledge, such as commodity production and special techniques.

Consider Zinan County of Hunan Province for an example. From 1979 to 1982, agricultural technical training developed rapidly. Almost 16,000 young and middle aged peasants (12 percent of this age group in the county) participated in 557 technical classes. At the end of 1983, the demand for these classes leveled off and interest began to shift to commercial productive techniques.

Peasant education began to place emphasis on practical technical programs while giving some attention to political education and literacy. Course content included agriculture, animal husbandry, fishery, forestry, industry, trade, transportation, architecture, and a variety of social services. The curriculum included classroom lectures, group learning, correspondence, broadcasting, TV, seminars, and independent studies. There were spare-time learning activities. Programs offered covered topics in higher education, secondary technical education, vocational education, the popularization of scientific knowledge, and literacy education.

Peasant vocational schools and peasant spare-time schools operated by townships are the main agencies through which programs are offered. Peasant secondary and higher technical education programs have become a focus in the suburban areas of large cities and relatively well-developed counties and townships. From 1981 to 1985, 100 million young and middle-aged peasants in China were trained in various learning schools or classes. Peasant education is playing an important part in the construction of material and spiritual civilization.

Adult Education in the Suburbs of Shanghai

The suburban area of the city of Shanghai is one area in China that has developed rapidly. In 1984 the total productive value of the 10 counties of the area reached 12 billion yuan, of which 6,470 million came from trade and industry. Purchasing commodities for export grew from 290 million in 1978 to 1,350 million in 1984. Agriculture and animal husbandry accounted for only 30 percent of the economic structure; second and third professions of the peasants accounted for 70 percent. In a Shanghai suburb, 450 thousand workers and 2.9 million peasants were targeted for adult education in county-run enterprises.

Presently, there are two types of peasant schools in the suburbs. One is aimed at training specialists and includes ten branch schools of Shanghai TV University, two county-run peasant secondary technical schools, ten branch schools or stations of the Central Agricultural Broadcasting School, and thirteen secondary technical schools operated by counties and bureaus. In addition, there are various higher or intermediate technical classes offered by TV secondary technical schools, party schools, correspondence programs, and contract training programs.

The other type of peasant school is aimed at basic education and technical education and includes 17 county-run cadre schools and township spare-time worker schools, 7 county or bureau agricultural technical training schools, and 260 county, bureau, or township spare-time schools and adult vocational schools.

In addition to the aforementioned schools and classes, suburban peasants also use the higher education self-study examination system as a means of upgrading their education. The self-study examination system is publicly supported and leads to national examinations and is an important measure in the education of the peasants.

Adult Education in Chuansha County

Among the ten suburban counties, Chuansha county of Shanghai operates exemplary adult educational programs. In 1985, of the 470 thousand participants in 10 counties, participants in Chuansha accounted for one-third. An adult educational system has been established that consists of programs run by counties, townships, and villages or enterprises. In this county there is 1 adult higher education college, 6 adult secondary technical schools, and 236 worker or peasant vocational schools operated by townships and bureaus. Radio, TV, correspondence, self-study, auxiliary teaching, classroom instruction, seminar, lecture, consulting, and demonstration are the methods of teaching. Subject matter includes worker technical education, remedial education, adult higher and secondary technical education, and social culture and life education.

Worker Technical Education. Chuansha is a county that has a variety of factories, and 140,000 peasants (54 percent of the total) are employed in factories. The total industrial production value in 1986 was 1.4 billion yuan. Industry has become a mainstay of Chuansha's economy. Most new industrial workers are peasants who have recently left their fields and have little systematic technical training. Most leaders of factories have no knowledge of modern management. The county recognizes the importance of encouraging workers and leaders to participate in vocational training, technical education, and management and to take classes in basic reading and writing skills.

The education of new workers and leaders is the responsibility of the industrial bureaus of the township government and the factories. Workers can participate in a variety of educational programs sponsored by the city, county, township, or enterprise, but most study in township secondary vocational schools. Workers engaged in technical jobs, such as electrical welding, stoking, and machine operations, usually participate in single-technique learning because they will receive a technical title (a symbol of promotion) after completing the tests.

Chuansha Adult Secondary Vocational School. This school was opened by the township government and ratified by the county Education Bureau. The township governor is also the principal of the school, which has its own campus and facilities. There are 5 full-time teachers and 53 part-time teachers. The funds to support the school come from the 20,000 yuan budget of the township government; a relatively small proportion of funds come from tuition fees. The purpose of the school is to train technicians in rudimentary skills, run secondary technical classes, and train part-time teachers and school administrators in the township.

The programs include techniques in agriculture, animal husbandry, veterinary medicine, accounting, quality control, mechanics, chemical engineering, textile production, electric welding, stoking, electric engineering, tractor repairing, sewing, and embroidery. Middle and high school equivalent education programs are also offered. Some programs are offered as spare-time classes, some on certain fixed days, half-days, or full days. Most of the participants, cadres, technicians, workers, members from specialized households, and young peasants have had at least a middle school education.

There are also some long-term and short-term classes. Short-term classes are aimed at training specialists, while long-term classes usually enroll young peasants, technicians, and workers, who, after one year's study, can reach the primary technical level. Textbooks and other teaching materials are usually those compiled by the province. Technologists or engineers from related fields are invited to teach. The school is on firm footing now, and every year there are about 3,000 participants in different programs.

Chuansha Correspondence Accounting School. This school was established in 1983 by the township Enterprises Industrial Bureau. The objectives are to prepare secondary accounting administrators and accountants for the factories in townships. The Advanced Finance and Economics Correspondence School of Minxin township of Shanghai is responsible for instruction within this school. Twelve courses are offered and include business writing in finance and economics, political economy, accounting in township enterprises, finance administration, enterprise management, economic law, philosophy, industrial accounting, auditing, economic activity analysis, foreign trade, and language.

The length of schooling is three and a half years. Correspondence independent study is the main method of teaching, with auxiliary face-to-face instruction one-half day per week. Currently, there are participants in all courses.

Remedial Education. Remedial education in Chuansha extends for up to nine years for all young and middle-aged peasants and twelve years for local cadres. (Remedial education refers to a special educational effort designed to help those young and middle-aged people who did not have secondary or elementary education.) The goal of remedial education is to help individuals attain the equivalency of a middle school education. In 1985, 160 individuals participated in spare-time secondary schools, 21,892 in middle school equivalent classes and 10,031 in high school equivalent classes. In a survey conducted in 1986, 82 percent of 12,000 young workers of county-run factories, and 40 percent of 28,163 workers in township factories had completed remedial education. Eighty percent of the township and bureau cadres finished high school equivalent remedial education.

Remedial education for the county- and township-level cadres is provided by the county-run schools. Worker-peasant teachers engage in full-time learning activities, village cadres are involved in spare-time remedial education conducted by vocational schools, and county-run enterprises train enterprise leaders. District spare-time schools also engage in remedial education for rural cadres.

The Chuansha County Cadre School was established by the county government and administered by the county Personnel Affairs Bureau and the Education Bureau. The deputy county governor is responsible for education and is also the principal. The school has its own buildings and 11 full-time teachers. Funding to support the school comes from the county budget (10,000 yuan annually) and from very modest tuition fees. Programs offered by this school include middle and high school equivalent courses, writing, Marxism, TV secondary technical courses, and party management. The length of schooling is one to two years. Participants in the programs number 2,000, and 1,000 have graduated and received high school diplomas.

Peasant Secondary and Higher Technical Education. For the past several years, the economic rate has increased in Chuansha county by 20 percent each year. If the county wants to maintain this rate, it must rely on specialists to increase productivity. There are not enough graduates from regular universities, and the county has to meet the need for specialists by providing adult secondary and higher technical education through TV and broadcasting universities, agricultural broadcasting schools, and peasant secondary technical schools.

Specialists with a two- to five-year college equivalent education are prepared by (1) contract-based university training, (2) county-run TV university branches, and (3) the higher education self-study examination system.

Secondary specialists are prepared by (1) county-run peasant secondary technical schools, (2) the Central Agricultural Broadcasting School, (3) TV secondary technical schools, and (4) the secondary technical self-study examination system.

The county-run TV universities admit only high school graduates, while secondary technical schools admit young peasants and cadres who have a diploma and who have also worked at least two years after graduation. The job placement of the graduates is not the responsibility of universities and schools. Instead, the working units that send the participants to school assign them new jobs if necessary. Funding support comes from the local county budget and tuition. In Chuansha county there is 1 adult higher education school and 6 secondary technical schools, with a working team of 196 individuals and a campus area of 15,000 square meters.

Chuansha Branch School of the Shanghai TV University. When the Shanghai TV University reopened in 1978, Chuansha county's leaders in the field of education and health took the opportunity to open TV classes and enroll participants in courses such as electronics, mathematics, physics, chemistry, and medicine. In 1983, after ratification by the county Education Bureau, the Chuansha Branch School of the Shanghai TV University was established and recorded with the Shanghai Higher Education Bureau. This school occupies an area of 22 mu (one mu equals approximately 700 square meters), and its building area is 3,000 square meters. A closed-circuit TV system provided by a World Bank Loan was installed. There are 254 full-time teachers, and 817 participants are enrolled.

Twenty-three programs—including medicine, mechanical engineering, electronics, chemistry, industrial management, finance and economics, Chinese, law, and cadre studies—are provided either on a spare-time, half-day, or a full-time basis to meet the needs of economic development in local communities.

Among the participants are workers, peasants, technicians, doctors, teachers, cadres, and managers. Some are admitted through examinations and some just audit classes. If an audit participant can go through the required courses and pass the final examinations, he or she is also eligible to get a graduate diploma from the Shanghai TV University. In eight years, the school has prepared 655 individuals for leadership in the county administration, schools, and enterprises.

The Chuansha Peasant Secondary Technical School. This school was established and ratified by the Shanghai municipal government in 1983. The purpose of this school is to prepare specialized rural secondary technicians to help commercialize and modernize the county's agriculture.

The school is owned by the county Agriculture Bureau, and daily operations are directed by the county Education Bureau. The director of the Agriculture Bureau serves concurrently as the principal, working with two full-time vice-principals and twenty-two full-time teachers.

The participants are either young peasants with two years' working experience and a middle school education or rural cadres and technicians with an education equivalent to middle school education. Usually, only those who are physically healthy and under the age of thirty are admitted.

Peasant applicants must receive permission from their working units and pass the city-administered entrance examination before they are admitted. Only those who get high scores are eligible. After graduation, the participants are granted a diploma and go back to their workplace. The government recognizes their education but is not responsible for job placement. Basically, cadres and technicians, as well as peasants, return to their original posts after graduation. The township government is responsible for assigning new jobs in rural technical fields to those city youths who originally came to the rural area to be re-educated during the Cultural Revolution.

The curriculum is similar to regular technical schools and is reviewed by the city Education Bureau and other concerned leading bodies. The purpose of the curriculum is to make sure that the participants will systematically learn theories, techniques, skills, and methods of solving practical problems. Five subjects are offered, including agriculture, vegetable production, horticulture, industrial management, and electronic automation. There are currently 158 participants in 5 classes, and 95 participants have graduated from this school.

The campus of the school is more than 20 mu, with a building area of 4,293 square meters. Facilities include a computer room, a lab, a reference room, and a library. There is also a dormitory for participants. Financing comes mainly from the budget of the city and county governments.

Chuansha Branch School of the Central Agricultural Broadcasting School. The Central Agricultural Broadcasting School is an agricultural technical school established jointly in 1981 by the Central Agriculture Department, the Central Fishery Department, the Husbandry Department, and the Education Department. The Chuansha Branch School is governed by the central and city branch schools and is managed by the county Committee of Worker Peasant Education. There are fifty classes offered in every township of the county. About 1,500 participants have enrolled in different programs over a nine-year period, and 256, have graduated. Programs offered include agricultural production and management, animal husbandry, fresh-water fishery, and vegetable and industry management. The length of study is three years. Diplomas are issued to those who have successfully completed the required courses and passed the nationally standardized examinations. The target groups considered for admission include county and township cadres who have not been trained through regular agricultural universities or colleges but have a middle school education; agricultural extension workers at agricultural science stations; peasant technicians who have already gained certain technical titles; and city youths who have come to live and work in rural areas.

Participants learn by listening every other day to the instructions broadcast by the Central People's Radio Station and again to the tapes provided by the county. They also receive one day a week face-to-face instruction provided by the school.

This form of adult education is highly appreciated by rural cadres, peasants, and other participants, for there is little expense, the results are satisfactory, and the problem of teacher shortage is avoided.

Social Culture and Life Education. With economic development, peasants become "richer and richer" with each passing year. Their aim in life is no longer "striving to fill the stomach" but enriching their spiritual life. "To seek fortune, knowledge, and entertainment" has already become their overall desire. To help enrich knowledge and spiritual life and make life more beautiful and enjoyable, the Chuansha Peasant Vocational School has already opened a variety of classes such as calligraphy, art, photography, wushu, sewing, cuisine, "fold" art, music, dancing, cosmetology, bridge, and "potted landscape."

The art class of Chengxiang Township Spare-Time Middle School was opened in 1981, and the period of study is two years. In every period there are twenty to forty participants, mainly young peasants and workers. Two groups of participants have already graduated. The class offers two specialties: mountain and water painting, and flower and bird painting. The instructions include sketching, imitation, creation, and mounting. After two years of study, participants can master the basic knowledge and skills. Some of them can even create their own paintings very successfully. Some even have won awards from county displays for their paintings.

Summary

The climate following the cultural revolution has given adult education great momentum, and it is believed that the development of adult education will promote continuing economic development in China.

Gu Genglin is vice-president of the Committee of Worker-Peasant Education of Chuansha County, Shanghai. He is also an executive member of the Shanghai Adult Education Research Society.

Education must serve the socialist construction, and the socialist construction must rely on education.

Worker Education

Zeng Yiziang, Li Guohua, Wu Tiaogeng

Chinese socialist enterprises are divided into state-owned, community-owned, and cooperatively invested enterprises (that is, enterprises invested by two or more agencies having different ownerships). At present, cooperatively invested enterprises in China are divided into two categories: (1) enterprises invested by state-owned agencies and, (2) community-owned agencies and enterprises invested by China and foreign agencies.

Industrial enterprises can be divided into large, medium-sized, and small-scale operations. The 1981 data from the State Statistics Bureau shows that among 380,000 industrial enterprises, less than 0.5 percent are large enterprises (1,500), 1 percent are medium-sized, and the remainder (over 98 percent) are small.

Worker education in enterprises is not only an important part of the national educational plan but also an indispensable foundation for the work of developing enterprises. The basic tasks are the development of the mind, preparation of specialists, raising the quality of workers, and modernization of socialist enterprises.

Worker education programs in enterprises in China today fall in two categories: degree and nondegree education programs. In degree programs, workers enroll in accredited worker universities operated by large and medium-sized enterprises, worker technical schools, and worker culture schools. After a long period of study, workers can get diplomas equivalent to those of regular universities, junior colleges, secondary specialized schools, and middle and high schools. Nondegree programs refer to short-term training designed to raise workers' level of competence and the productivity of the enterprises.

The content of worker education in enterprises includes politics, reading and writing, management, and technology. There are three forms of learning: (1) spare-time learning, (2) semi-off-job learning, and (3) off-job (released time) learning. With the approval of the government, worker institutions can admit students from the general public to certain enterprises. Graduates from these institutions will be assigned jobs by these enterprises. Funds supporting education come mainly from the enterprises that run them. This kind of education is referred to as worker preparation education.

Legislation has recognized that worker education is an important form of education. In the early days after the founding of New China, the main task of worker education was literacy. From 1953, when the first Five-Year Plan began, worker education in enterprises became more sophisticated. In the seventeen years following the founding of New China, worker education developed rapidly as a result of the encouragement provided by government policy and the strong leadership provided by enterprises. The illiteracy of 8.7 million people was "wiped out": 2.3 million workers reached elementary education levels, 960,000 workers reached middle and high school education levels, and 200,000 workers graduated from higher educational institutions. In 1965 there were over 17 million participants in worker educational institutions.

During the Cultural Revolution, worker education was seriously damaged and practically came to a standstill but was restored in the late 1970s. The Decision on the Strengthening of Worker Education was promulgated by the government in 1981. The 1985 Decision on the Reformation of the Education System provided this guiding principle: "Education must serve the socialist construction, and socialist construction must rely on education." Worker education has entered a new stage in terms of scale, content, and methodology. According to the 1986 statistics, there are 1.5 million participants in various worker higher education institutions.

Worker Education in Large Enterprises

Large enterprises refer to those industrial entities that have mass production, a large labor force, and good equipment. They are the backbone of modernization and the lifeline of the nation's economy. Worker education in large enterprises sets the example for medium-sized and small-scale enterprises.

A description of worker education in one plant will provide a more comprehensive understanding of an ideal program.

Located in Changchun city in Jilin province, the First Auto Plant, one of the largest enterprises in China, produces mainly heavy trucks. The construction of the plant began in 1953 and was brought on line in 1956. Currently, there are 50,000 employees, and the plant produces 30,000 trucks annually.

In 30 years, the plant has turned out 1.2 million trucks. Its contribution includes its invaluable experience to the technical development of China's auto industry and the specialist worker force the industry has developed.

Along with the development of the plant, worker education expanded. For five successive years from 1982 to 1986, this plant won the Model Unit in Worker Education Award within the auto industry system. And in 1985 it won The Best Intelligence Development Cup.

In its early years, the First Auto Plant faced a serious problem. While equipment, production processes, and management were quite advanced for the time, the skills of the workers were inadequate. Among the 700 cadres, most had transferred from other professions and did not know auto-making techniques, lacked the experience of managing mass production, and possessed a minimal level of education. Of approximately 1,300 technicians, only 5 percent held the title of engineer. The remainder were young graduates of universities or secondary technical schools. Twenty-five percent of the 12,000 workers were experienced, and the remaining 75 percent were young peasants and middle school and high school graduates.

If the First Auto Plant were to develop, the leaders realized that the problem of education had to be resolved. They organized a program to train workers and adopted this principle: "The construction of the plant, production preparation, and training of the employees must proceed simultaneously." Under the principle of "learning what relates to what one is doing," the plant sent many of its employees to learn either abroad or at home in other auto plants. Short-term training classes aimed at increasing job competence were also opened. A learning climate was established at the plant within a few years, and everybody, from managers to workers, was actively involved in learning. In 1954 spare-time institutions were established and included worker basic educational schools, secondary technical schools, and night colleges.

Worker education in the plant guaranteed the successful construction of the plant within three years and the beginning of the production of the Liberation Truck in July 1956. This learning climate is present today. In just over thirty years, a comprehensive training system has been formed, which is discussed in the following sections.

Inservice Worker Degree Education. This is conducted by the four institutions of the plant: the Worker University, the Worker Secondary Technical School, the Worker Spare-Time Technical School, and the Worker Spare-Time Secondary School.

The Worker University. The university consists of five units: the full-time university working unit (four years), the spare-time university working unit, the TV university working station, the correspondence university working station, and the periodical education working station. The university has 193 teachers and staff and an enrollment of 2,000 participants. There are 16 disciplines, including mechanical engineering, enterprise management, electronic automation of industrial enterprise, accounting, statistics, auto transportation engineering, record management, Chinese, science information, library management, and industrial and civic architecture.

In the past 33 years, the university has graduated 1,700 workers, who make up 50 percent of the plant workers. These graduates are integrated into and enhance the quality of the entire work force.

The Worker Secondary Technical School. This school has been in existence for over thirty years. Half of the secondary technical graduates in the plant are prepared by this school. Presently, there are 520 participants in the specialities of machine manufacturing, electronic automation in industrial enterprise management, and civic and industrial architecture.

The Worker Spare-Time Technical School. This school was opened in 1985, and its purpose is to systematically raise the theory and skill levels of workers who hold the third technical level rank and above, as well as to train workers in the applications of new technology. Currently, 460 participants are learning skills in fields such as electrotechnics, welding, piping, and machine manufacturing.

The Worker Spare-Time Secondary School. This school has existed for more than thirty years, and its purpose is to raise the educational level of workers and to prepare participants for the Worker Secondary Technical School and the Worker University. Presently, there are more than 1,000 participants.

Degree Education for Future Workers. To prepare for development, the plant makes large investments in the education of future workers, namely through the master's program of the Auto Research Institute of the plant, the Higher Technical School of Changchun Auto Industry, the Auto Industry School, the Technical School, and the Vocational School.

Master's Program of the Auto Research Institute. In order to prepare higher-level specialists, the Auto Research Institute of the plant began to recruit master's-level students in 1984. At present, there are twenty-six graduate students in the two disciplines of auto and internal combustion engineering. Four graduates directed by the outstanding expert Guo Kenghue have entered the stage of writing their theses.

The Higher Technical School of Changchun Auto Industry. This school, founded in 1984, is responsible for the training of junior specialists and technicians with practical skills. Four urgently needed disciplines have been provided: machine manufacturing, electronic computer software, automotive experimental techniques, and enterprise management. Currently, there are 370 participants, and plans are to enlarge enrollment to 1,000 before 1990.

The Auto Industry School. Operated by the plant, this school trains secondary-level technicians in occupations such as machine manufacturing, enterprise management, finance and accounting, and statistics. Currently, this school has 300 participants.

The Technical School. This school trains intermediate skilled workers for the plant. There are fifteen disciplines, including electrotechnics, welding, molding, forging, meter, hearthandling, and machine manufacturing. The annual enrollment is 400, and there are now 1,200 participants.

The Vocational School. Students in this school are middle school graduates, and three years of schooling are required for admission. The school prepares intermediate skilled workers and staff for state ownership and community ownership enterprises within the plant. Programs include lathe turning, milling, sharpening, welding, piping, cooking, drawing, and trade. At present, there are 900 students.

Nondegree Education of the First Auto Plant. Nondegree education is the major portion of worker education in the First Auto Plant. This short-term training is efficient, less time consuming, and practical.

The training office, the Electronic Education Office, and the Young Worker Political School are the "line" offices that provide training; staff support is given by 100 staff members. Apart from the central plant's branch factories and administrative managers, there are 30 worker education offices or institutions, with 150 staff members and teachers. The work of these offices or institutions is directed by the Technical Training Department.

In recent years there has been a focus on the training of cadres from the plant and its branch factories. The purpose of the training is to expand and upgrade cadres' knowledge of decision making, selling, quality control, and economic laws and regulations. In 1984 the State Economy Committee stipulated that managers and directors of large and medium-sized enterprises must take examinations in policy, guidelines, and enterprise management. The ratings received by the cadres from the First Auto Plant are higher on average than those received by the whole country and are at the top in the machine industry category. Six cadres won the Supreme Award and the Excellent Award.

Advanced engineer education at the plant has a long history. It focuses on new products, improvement of techniques, introduction of new technology and equipment, application of modern management approaches, and upgrading of worker knowledge skills. This system has been highly commended by the National Science Committee and the Chinese Continuing Engineering Education Association.

Now that scientific management of enterprises is being stressed, the knowledge structure and job competence of the managers at all levels should undergo great changes. Under this mandate, the plant has developed and implemented a training program for managers from a dozen branch factories and workshops. The program begins with basic knowledge of relevant professions and then develops competencies in modern management. A noteworthy advance is the creation of a seminar in which learning is combined with the application of new management approaches.

Worker Education in Medium-Sized Enterprises

An example of worker education in a medium-sized enterprise is found in the program of the Shanghai Bulb Factory.

The Shanghai Bulb Factory has a history of more than 70 years. The products of this factory include kinescope, electron tubing, tungsten filament, and molybdenum filament. There are 2,849 employees, and worker education in the factory is administered by the Education Office, which is responsible to the manager. The office has 1 administrator and 5 staff members.

Education content is based on the practical needs of the factory and the worker and is conducted by the factory itself or by institutions or agencies outside the factory.

Factory Worker Education. The factory provides nine categories of education, as discussed below.

English Class. This class uses two half working days per week to teach English to engineers and technicians. There are twenty-two engineers and associate engineers participating in the class. The length of the course is one and a half years, during which time no wages or fringe benefits are deducted.

Guidance Class for Secondary Technical Self-Study. The purpose of this class is to help self-study learners intending to take examinations. This class is designed for leaders of workshops and offices to help them raise their education and management levels. Currently, there are thirty-three participants, and the class uses two half working days per week. According to the regulations developed by the Shanghai Education Bureau, those who want to get their diplomas must finish and pass the following twelve courses: political economy, introduction to economy, management mathematics, principles of accounting, Chinese, philosophy, calculation techniques, basic computer knowledge and skill, introduction to economic law, basic statistics, industrial enterprise management, and marketing. Nine participants received their diplomas at the end of 1986. The remaining twenty-four will take examinations in the first half of 1987.

Quality-Control Class. The purpose of this class is to help the team and group leaders from production lines maintain and raise the quality of products. There are 190 participants now, who also spend two half working days per week in study. Eighty-nine percent of these participants have passed the examination conducted by the Shanghai Quality-Control Association. The class is taught by the quality controllers of the factory.

Spare-Time High School Completion Self-Study Class. This class is designed to meet the needs of young workers, and spare-time learning is the main learning form. Teachers of the factory technical school are invited to teach the class in their spare time. In 1985 there were 128 participants in the spring session and 133 in the fall session. Thirty percent of the spring class and 41 percent of the fall class have passed the examination administered by the Shanghai Education Bureau.

Spare-Time High School Completion Class. In response to the requirement, 3 of these classes were formed in 1985. There are 119 participants enrolled in the opening classes. During the first half of the year, 32 workers participated in high school Chinese and political classes, and in the second half of the year, 87 participated in high school Chinese, mathematics, and history classes. The classes are taught by teachers either invited from outside the factory or from the factory technical school.

Spare-Time Middle School Completion Class. Again in response to the state requirement, 1 physics class and 3 chemistry classes were opened in 1985 and enrolled 179 workers. All learning experiences are organized in the spare-time format, and teachers come from factory-run spare-time middle schools that have already been accredited by the Shanghai Putuo District Education Bureau.

Off-Job Middle School Completion Class. Two such classes were opened in 1985, and 789 participants were released from their jobs and studied intensively for 3 months.

Energy Resource Class. In order to save energy and manage resources, the factory opened this class for workshop leaders, heads of offices, and energy managers of the factory. From 1984 the factory has spent one week per year teaching energy management. Teaching materials are compiled by the leaders of the factory Energy Resource Office. Instruction is closely combined with practice, and the class is popular with participants.

Intermediate Technical Training Class. The factory opened 4 such classes in 1985, 3 electric vacuum technical classes and 1 tungsten and molybdenum technical class. There are 136 participants who use one month each year (the time set aside for equipment maintenance) to learn the courses and skills stipulated by the Chinese Electronic Industry Department. Instructions are provided by teachers from the factory technical school. At the end of the courses, examinations are conducted. Wages and fringe benefits are continued for all participants in classes.

Worker Education Outside the Factory. Worker education is also provided by institutions or agencies outside the factory, as discussed in the following sections.

Worker Higher Education Entrance Preparation Class. In 1985, 171 young workers (under the age of 30) enrolled in such classes and studied in their spare time to pass entrance examinations of worker universities. The factory provided funds and enlisted Puyun High School to do the training. Three high school review classes were formed, and after 4 months of intensive study, 56 participants passed the examinations and were admitted by worker universities. During their study, participants received wages regularly and the factory provided 60 yuan scholarships and 18 yuan medical fees for each.

Electric Vacuum Two-Year College Equivalent Class. The factory required more specialists in electric vacuum devices, so it contracted with the Worker University of the Shanghai Meter and Electronic Communication Bureau to open an electric vacuum device class at the two-year college level. Through examinations, forty-six participants have been admitted. The period of study is three years, using working time. On graduation participants will receive junior college equivalent diplomas.

Enterprise Management Class at a Two-Year College Level. The factory enlisted the Jingan District Spare-Time University to open an enterprise management class. The period of schooling is three years, during which time the participants use two paid working days per week to study. There are twenty-six participants.

Quality Control Short Courses. The factory contracts with the Putuo District Spare-Time University to open nine quality control classes. The time of study is 4 months, during which time participants use 2 paid half working days. There were 348 participants trained in 1985. Diplomas are issued to those who pass the examinations at the end of the course.

Vocational High School Class. Cooperating with some high schools, the factory opened classes in machinery, electric vacuum device, electronic meters, and hydraulic electricity. There are 187 students who are all middle school graduates. The schools are responsible for the basic education and administration of the teaching and learning process, and the factory is only responsible for technical instruction and internship. After three years of study, vocational high school diplomas are issued to students by the Shanghai Education Bureau and third grade technique titles are issued by the factory. Job placement is the responsibility of the factory. During internship, each student gets a 1.5 yuan support fee per day.

Two Regular Schools. In addition to the above-mentioned classes, the Shanghai Bulb Factory has two regular schools to conduct worker education.

The Worker Technical School. This school was founded in the 1960s and has 201 teachers and staff members. It has a campus of 2,200 square meters. Two disciplines have been taught in the school: mechanical and electric vacuum device. In 1985 there were 160 students. The school recruits middle school graduates and trains them as technical workers for the factory. As of 1986, the school had trained 748 workers for various posts in the factory. Many of the graduates have become integral to production, and 16 have become cadres in workshops and offices.

The Spare-Time Middle School. This school offered middle school curriculum according to the outlines of the state. Since 1979 the school has opened 35 classes during spare time and working time, and 1,690 young workers have participated in these classes. Most instructors were invited from the Technical School, and some were technicians. Most of the workers used their spare time or two half working days to study. There were 2,267 participants in 1985, and only 260 (11 percent) were full-time learners. Counting the 160 students of the Technical School, there were 2,343 participants, making up 85 percent of all the workers of the factory. Fifty-one classes have been opened. In 1986 this school finished its tasks and was closed down.

Worker Education in Small Enterprises

Small enterprises are ones with less than 500 employees, and worker educational programs in these enterprises have their own particular features. As an example, consider the worker education programs of the Shanghai High Pressure Oil Pump Plant.

The Shanghai High Pressure Oil Pump Plant produces oil motors and high-pressure shaft piston pumps. There are 484 employees, and this plant has been seriously upholding the government mandate concerning worker education. To encourage workers to participate in learning activities, leaders communicate the following ideas: (1) Workers are the masters of the plant; (2) the development of the plant can only rely on the workers; and (3) the plant should take care of the ideology, culture, and living problems of the workers. Based on these precepts, the plant conducts the education of its workers. A systematic educational attempt has been made to attack the problem of "three lows and one lack," that is, the education level, the skills of the workers, and the management level are low, and the factory lacks technicians and specialists.

Based on a survey of the education and skill levels of all workers, the plant has developed training plans for everybody. It is difficult for small enterprises to provide education and training because of limited resources. The plant has adopted various forms to educate and train its workers, which include on-job and off-job learning, basic cultural education, technical training, cadre special education, and worker special training.

The education and personnel offices of the factory discover and train talented people in special fields. When they find the kind of people they want (usually workers who are devoted, hard working, and have a strong desire to learn), they have the worker complete an "expectation form." This form includes information on the special skills or knowledge of the worker, his or her interests and expectations, as well as ways the worker expects to bring these expectations to fruition, including what contribution the worker wants to make to the plant. The form is placed in the worker's file in the personnel office, along with an ability development card, which will be referred to during training.

In considering jobs and roles of the workers, the plant takes different measures in conducting worker education and training, as follows:

1. For production line workers, emphasis is given to basic education and training. Promising young workers are also chosen to participate in programs offered by TV universities and worker universities.

2. For leaders of working teams and groups from the production line, four working hours per week are provided, which are divided into two periods. Workers study such topics as labor organization, ideological and political work, quality, equipment, resource development, and basic management knowledge.

3. For technicians and engineers, a system of five working days and one learning day has been implemented. On the learning day, participants learn foreign languages in the morning and study their own disciplines in the afternoon. University professors are invited regularly to teach courses, and workers participate in domestic or foreign conferences.

4. For managers at all levels, opportunities are provided for participation in various enterprise management classes and meetings. Managers are also encouraged to attend TV lectures offered by the Shanghai TV University.

In the past several years, 58 employees have graduated as senior and junior students, 156 have graduated from secondary technical schools and high schools, and 87 have been trained as middle-level skilled workers, high skilled workers, or technicians. Through special training, 4 workers have become cadres at the bureau and city levels. Many of the participants in special programs have become cadres in the field of technical, production, and management of the plant.

Leaders of the Shanghai High Pressure Oil Pump Plant believe that worker education programs have the same importance as production and quality control and have been trying to increase the capacity for education at the plant. Technicians and engineers of the plant are invited to teach part-time. Teaching materials are compiled by specialists in the plant. Workers are encouraged to share more jobs to enable their fellow workers to participate in learning activities. The problem of space is solved by rearranging facilities. Two rooms of eighty square meters each have been set aside as classrooms in the plant.

The example of the Shanghai High Pressure Oil Pump Plant shows that small enterprises can run worker education programs well and that worker education in small enterprises can serve the development of workers and of production.

Zeng Yiziang is director of the Council of the Worker Education Committee of the Chinese Auto Engineering Society.

Li Guohua is a member of the Council of the Worker Education Association of the Chinese Electronic Industry.

Wu Tiaogeng is head of the Education Office of Shanghai High Pressure Oil Pump Plant.

The party school adheres to the principle of "taking the whole society as our classroom and running an open door education," which makes concrete research and investigation the major content of each training course.

Cadre Education

Lin Jixiang, Zhou Maosheng

The term *cadre* in China refers to administrative or managerial personnel as well as to other professionals and technical personnel who maintain the status of civic servants within the following working bodies: the Central Committee of the Chinese Communist Party (CCCCP), the National People's Congress, the Chinese People's Political Consultative Conference (CPPCC), and public or government organizations at all levels above village and town or subdistricts in the cities. The term also refers to those leading personnel within enterprises and businesses owned by the public. The staff within primary and secondary schools are also referred to as cadres. In this chapter, which focuses on cadre training and education, the term *cadre* refers only to the leading personnel and administrative personnel working at all levels of government organizations.

Background

There have been several periods of development in the history of cadre education in China. During World War II, when the Worker Peasant Red Army successfully reached Yanan after the Long March, under the leadership of the Chinese Communist Party (CCP), base camps were established to train cadres for the Anti-Japanese War. At that time cadres were badly needed to fight in the war.

In responding to this need, the Central Department of Cadre Education was established in October 1938, with Zhang Wentian, then general secretary of CCCCP, as the person in charge. A "Decisions for On-Job Training for Cadres" was made, which stipulated theories, policies, professional skills, and the curriculum. Several well-known institutions for cadre training were set up, including the Chinese People's Anti-Japanese Military and Political University (Linbiao, president), Shanbei College (Cheng Fangwu, president), and the Lu Xun Art Academy (Zhou Yang, president). In May 1939, the Central Committee decided to transfer some cadres from northern China and other places to Yanan to be trained. From these cadres came new teachers. Many well-known leaders compiled teaching materials and gave lectures to the trainees. Mao Zedong wrote reading materials for cadre training, such as "The Chinese Revolution and the Communist Party" and "On Persistant War." He also gave lectures under special topics such as "The Second Imperialist War" and "Reform Our Study." Liu Shaoqi wrote and presented a lecture entitled "On Self-Cultivation of Members of the Communist Party." Some textbooks from Russia were also translated as teaching materials. Because of the war, resources such as housing, teachers, textbooks, and paper were difficult to obtain, and the learning conditions were very hard. Yet despite all these problems, many cadres were clear about the purpose of their study and studied diligently. Cadre education and training at that time developed thousands of talented persons for leadership in the Anti-Japanese and Liberation War. These people became the backbone for the socialist construction of society after the liberation of the entire country.

After the establishment of New China, the country turned from war to economic construction. In order for cadres to master the knowledge and skills needed to pursue construction and management, with which they were unfamiliar, and to help them meet the demands of socialist construction, another major development occurred in cadre education: school completion.

In 1953 CCCCP issued Directives on Strenghtening the Education for Cadres, which required that party committees at all levels to pay attention to the education of cadres and to the enhancement of their leadership. During this period, a large number of schools such as cadre spare-time culture schools, worker and peasant accelerated middle schools, and cadre off-job remedial schools sprang up in different areas of the country. According to the incomplete statistics in the second half of 1955, there were 3,546 cadre spare-time culture schools nationally, with over 1 million people participating. There also were 256 cadre off-job schools, with 80,470 participants. At the same time, many young cadres were transferred into full-time study at universities.

After the CCP's Third Plenary Session of the Eleventh Conference in 1978, the turmoil caused by the ten-year Cultural Revolution was over, and cadre education, which was at a standstill during this period, became revitalized. Along with the shift of the party's policy on the "construction of the four modernizations," the party required cadres to be more revolutionary, informed, and specialized. The party considered it of strategic significance to train cadres on a large scale in order to raise the quality of their leadership and to build a large number of professional personnel for the construction of a modern socialist society. Accordingly, cadre education was reshaped as it entered a new period of development.

During this period, the CCCCP and the State Council made a series of decisions that provided instructions to strengthen cadre education. These included: Suggestions for Strengthening the Work of Cadre Education (by the Department of Organization and the Department of Propaganda of the CCP); Decisions on the Work of Cadre Education Within the Party and Government Organizations of the Central Committee (by the CCCCP and the State Council); Decisions on the Regularization of Party Schools Education (by the CCCCP); and The Principles of the Program for Nationwide Cadre Training (by the Department of Organization and the CCCCP). A national conference was held on cadre training in December 1983, which set forth the same idea: that to meet new demands of the society, cadre education and training must be consolidated and training made regular and systematic.

The basic purpose of cadre education was to improve all cadres' understanding of Marxist theory, make them professionals, raise their formal educational level, and help them demonstrate leadership and management abilities. Under this plan, cadres would be more competent leaders in the party and country, loyal to socialism, and recognized as professionals.

The documents also stipulated that cadre education should be brought into line with the state plan and that all cadres in the working bodies of the Central Committee should be trained in stages and in groups. Further, cadres should receive six months of training every three years, to be carried out within the cadre's appointment. Those who were proficient in their learning and in their work would be promoted first; during off-job training, employees would get the same pay and treatment as those in service.

The documents required that within the party and central governmental organizations, cadres under age forty with an education level below middle school should complete their middle school education within two or three years; those who already had a middle school education but lacked professional skills should reach the secondary specialized or junior college level.

The content of training, which formerly stressed Marxist-Leninist theories, shifted to the present comprehensive training, which stresses that political theories, science and culture, and professional skills are equally important. The target audience for training, which previously was mainly assigned leaders and cadres in the party and government services, is now widespread, and training is available to reserve cadres as well as assigned leaders and cadres in all trades and professions. The training institutions, which were mainly party and cadre schools, now include a variety of other forms such as self-study, correspondence education, TV and radio education, and spare-time forms of learning. Based on the spirit of the party's instructions on education, a party school training system has been gradually established for cadres in the party and government offices and for propaganda cadres. The following were also established: (1) the cadre school system for administrators and professional personnel in government; (2) the university and college system of special courses for training technical and managerial personnel or formal enrollment in the college of administration and management; and (3) the spare-time learning system for cadre education, including TV, broadcasting, correspondence, and self-study examinations. Thus, with a well-organized administrative structure and a system of standards, a nationwide network for cadre training has been formed.

In December 1984, to further strengthen the leadership in cadre education, a committee on cadre education at the party's central level and at the provincial, autonomous areas and city levels was established. The work of cadre education is thus ensured.

Cadre education during this new period was forcefully advanced and has become a well-established system. By the end of 1984, there were 8,677 party and cadre schools and 1,854 higher and secondary specialized schools responsible for cadre training. In 1984 almost 1.5 million cadres were trained in these schools, and a similar number were learning in spare-time universities, higher correspondence schools, and broadcasting and TV universities and were preparing for the higher level self-study examinations. Over 2 million students participated in short-term political and professional training. In 1985 many cadres participated in high school completion programs, and 1,500 graduated from multicourse and single-course programs. There were another 460,000 who graduated from middle school programs.

Party Schools: An Important Area of Cadre Education

Party schools at all levels in China are schools under the direct leadership of the CCP. The purpose of party schools is to train leaders for the party and government. These schools are an important component of adult education in China. After the Third Plenary Session of the Eleventh Conference of the CCP, party schools at the central level were reconstituted and party schools at other levels followed. By the end of 1985, there were 2,700 newly established or reestablished party schools from the central level to the local level, including provinces, cities, districts, and counties. In 1983 the CCCCP decided to standardize the curriculum in party schools. The fundamental task of party schools at all levels was to provide the party's cadres with the basic theories of Marxism-Leninism, Mao Zedong thought, policies and principles of the party, and the scientific and professional knowledge necessary to build a modern society. From this time on, cadres of the party and the government who held leading posts in provinces or districts would be trained in party schools at the central level, while those cadres in counties would be trained in party schools at the district, city, and county level. Thus, party schools gradually gained a unified system of classes and grades, course content, teaching materials, and examination.

Cadre Education in the Shanghai Party School

On Sanmen Road at the northeast corner of Shanghai stands the best school for cadre training in Shanghai: the Shanghai Party School. Most of Shanghai's cadres above the middle level and reserved cadres at the bureau level have been educated here.

This party school was established in July 1949, in the early days of liberation. After the Gang of Four had been convicted, the school was rebuilt in November 1977. From its rebuilding to the end of 1985, 14,000 cadres have been trained. Some participants come from other provinces and cities far from Shanghai. Many newly-appointed leaders of the Shanghai Party Committee and government have also been trained here. Among the presidents of the Shanghai Party School are the former secretaries of the Party Committee of Shanghai: Liu Xiao, Chen Pixian, Liu Changsheng, Ke Qingshi, Peng Chong, and Chen Guodong. The present president, Rui Xingwen, is also secretary of the Shanghai Party Committee. Currently, the Shanghai Party School has a faculty and staff of more than 440, which includes over 160 teachers and researchers and several dozen librarians. A number of professors and researchers are outstanding figures in their fields. There are 9 teaching and research groups and a theory study group in the school that covers courses ranging from philosophy, political economics, scientific socialism, the history of the CCP, the development of the CCP, literature and history, the science of management, the science of administration, and law. The school also publishes a magazine, *Forum of the Party and Politics,* and a school journal, *Newsletter of the Shanghai Party School.*

The Shanghai Party School also has a close relationship and a cooperative program with the other 71 party schools in the district, county, and bureau levels in Shanghai, and a city network of cadre education in party schools has been formed. The total campus area of these schools covers 160,000 square meters. The schools can accommodate 10,000 nonresidential participants and 5,000 residential participants.

From 1984 to 1985, 25,000 persons were enrolled. The Shanghai Party School is ranked as a higher education institution but with its own specialized audience. This audience is composed of leaders and reserved leaders at the bureau level of the party and government, including leaders below the bureau level of the party, government, industry, and civic enterprises. Teachers of party schools and cadres for theoretical and political work are trained at the Shanghai Party School.

There are three major classes and grades of the Shanghai Party School, as follows:

1. *Training classes.* The period of schooling is two to three years. Participants should be under age forty and have more than a three-year college degree. They should have at least five years of work experience and are required to possess good political qualifications. Courses offered are in Marxist philosophy, political economics, scientific socialism, the history of the CCP, the development of the CCP, leadership arts, economics management, administration management, world economics, law, and modern history of China.

2. *Theory classes.* The period of schooling is two to three years. The purpose is to train theory-oriented teachers of party schools and cadres working in propaganda. Participants must be party members under the age of thirty-five, have a degree above the three-year college level and have had three years of work experience. Courses offered are philosophy, political economics, the history of the CCP, and scientific socialism.

3. *Refresher classes.* The period of schooling varies from six months to one year. Leading personnel in the party and government at the bureau level or the level directly under the bureau take required courses. In addition, short-term rotating training and research classes are also offered by the Shanghai Party School.

Cadres at all levels studying in the Shanghai Party School are selected through strict requirements set by the Personnel Department. Care is taken because most cadres will be assigned to leading posts after completing their studies in the Party School. The Party School recruits participants through recommendation and examination. Candidates can be nominated by their units or apply themselves. After checking a recommendation, a standard examination is administered, and those who qualify are selected.

The faculty of the Shanghai Party School, as models exemplifying the virtues of the party, possess a relatively high academic level of theory and research. It is necessary for them to be outstanding Communists. They are selected by the Shanghai Party Committee from students graduating from universities and from the university graduate school faculty. Those who have been selected are usually of good character and scholarship. Teachers from other departments are also transferred to the Party

School to strengthen its faculty. Experts from various fields, outstanding professors, and leading personnel of the party and governmental units are invited to give lectures at the Shanghai Party School.

The secretary of the Shanghai Party Committee, the mayor, and other leading persons of various departments often give speeches and reports at the Shanghai Party School. Much emphasis has been given to the use of case studies in teaching activities. Participants are encouraged to collect cases, write reports on the cases, and then analyze and discuss them among their colleagues.

The Party School adheres to the principle of "taking the whole society as our classroom and running an open-door education" and thus makes concrete research and investigation the major content of each training course. The projects for research and investigation usually arise from problems and issues encountered in practical work. Such investigations of problems usually involve three steps: (1) making a questionnaire of interests in research and investigation to clarify the problem (lecture on special topics such as methods for Social Investigation, How to Initiate Effective Social Investigation, and Introduction to Methods of Quantitative Analysis are given at this first step to familiarize students with social science and natural science methodology and computer analysis); (2) investigating the practical problems identified by sending out questionnaires or administering statistical evaluation forms; and (3) writing a research and investigation report providing consultative suggestions to the related units.

The Shanghai Party School is not only a place for training cadres but also for testing them. The procedure of examination includes oral defense by the student. The examining committee is composed of experts, scholars, and leading persons from related units who follow formal procedures and requirements in the examination.

China is now trying to accelerate attainment of modernization goals and the carrying out of an open-door policy. Shanghai is the largest open-door city and the center of the economy. Exchange activities between foreign countries—such as Romania, Yugoslavia, Korea, Hungary, Italy, Germany, France, Japan, and Somalia—and the cadres and scholars in the Shanghai Party School are carried out daily. Presently, a new modern teaching facility for the Shanghai Party School is under construction in the southwest of Shanghai for the purpose of meeting the increasing demands of cadre training.

Lin Jixiang is department head of Human Resource Development of the Shanghai Science Cadre Bureau.

Zhou Maosheng is a cadre in the Shanghai Personnel Bureau.

Social educational activities are sure to lead to social effects; adults can develop their abilities, improve their personalities, and give full play to their talents.

Adult Social Education

Zhu Yuancheng

A Description

In China social education refers to any organized educational activities outside of school and is a part of cultural activities offered to the public. There are four types of popular cultural activity systems that include social education. The first two types specifically serve adults.

The first type serves the general public. Facilities of this type include municipal art galleries, district cultural centers, neighborhood or town cultural stations, relevant libraries, and sports stadiums.

The second type is sponsored by trade unions and serves all cadres and workers in the fields of education, health, and industrial and mineral enterprises. Activities are located in city worker's palaces, district worker's clubs, union libraries, and sports fields.

The third type belongs to the Communist Youth League system and serves young people. The Youth Palace is the center for the activities.

The fourth type serves children. There are both municipal and district children's palaces and children's homes in neighborhoods.

Funds for popular cultural activities come from the following sources: (1) governmental appropriations; (2) appropriations, financial support, donations, and subsidies from state and commune enterprises, and (3) activity fees. Popular cultural activities organized by the government are mainly supported by governmental allocation. Activities run by trade unions are usually funded by all three sources. The relatively abundant government funds for social education, augmented by support from both the Trade Union of the People's Republic of China and the Shanghai Trade Union, have enabled worker's cultural palaces, clubs, libraries, and sports facilities to develop greatly in recent years and become the base for popular cultural activities.

The Shanghai Municipal Government, for example, has built 20 regional cultural centers, which occupy an area of 54,000 square meters. The Shanghai Trade Union has built 18 district- and bureau-level cultural palaces and clubs, which occupy a floor space of 194,000 square meters, including a construction area of 51,000 square meters.

At the township and neighborhood levels, the Shanghai Municipal Government has built 201 cultural centers and stations, 364 libraries, and more than 1,200 sports fields. Also, at this level the Shanghai Trade Union has set up 1,000 worker's clubs, about 8,000 grass-roots libraries, and more than 8,000 grass-roots sports fields. These facilities serve a city of 11 million people.

Under the administration of all trade unions throughout the country, there are more than 20,000 worker's cultural palaces and clubs, more than 140,000 libraries, and more than 10,000 full-time personnel engaged in administering these activities.

Through the following figures provided by Putuo district in Shanghai, the reader can have a general idea of how the trade union system carries out popular cultural activities in the grass-roots units. The Putuo district is one of twelve districts in Shanghai. In the Putuo district there are 99 enterprises and units administered by the 12 city and district bureaus that employ 212,000 workers. The grass-roots trade unions in these enterprises and units have the following resources:

- 88 clubs or workers' homes, occupying an area of 14,825 square meters
- 99 libraries, occupying an area of 5,605 square meters with a collection of 549,000 books
- 352 sports teams, with about 10,000 participants
- 96 troupes of performing artists, with about 1,500 volunteer participants
- 327 spare-time hobby groups, with about 10,000 participants.

The statistics of the Putuo district can be duplicated in other districts. In Shanghai, there is one square meter of club or library activity space for every ten workers. There is an average of two and a half books per worker. And at least one out of every ten workers takes part in sports, performance, art, and hobby group activities.

The Shanghai Worker's Cultural Palace

Founded on October 1, 1950, and situated at the center of Shanghai east of the People's Square, the Shanghai Worker's Cultural Palace is a comprehensive cultural facility under the direct sponsorship of the Shanghai Trade Union. It occupies an area of 2,000 square meters. It has 3 theaters, 2 exhibition halls, a collection of 200,000 books, 4 reading rooms, a large recreation hall, and more than 10 rehearsal rooms.

The administrative system of the palace consists of a director under whom are the divisions of propaganda, book reading, art, cultural cultivation, TV, literature, and theater; each division carries out its own popular cultural activities. The 1986 adult education activities are discussed below.

Exhibitions. Altogether, twenty-six exhibitions have been held, which included the Display of Seven-City Worker Wood Pictures, the Shanghai-Anhui Nine-Mines Worker Drawing Show, the Exhibition of Scenery Drawing by the Association of Amateur Fine Arts Workers, the Western Style Drawing Show, and the Exhibition of Photos. These exhibitions draw large crowds; for example, the Shanghai Huangpu District Nameplate and High Quality Commodity and the Down Coats Fairs were attended by about 1,500,000 persons.

Lecture Series. There have been altogether 34 lectures and reports attended collectively by 34,000 persons. The speakers are usually famous scholars and authorities and thus attract a large audience. The lectures and reports are usually given in the mornings and targeted at cadres, who are engaged in political and ideological work in various manufacturing enterprises. Workers who are interested can also attend. Topics of various lectures and reports have included the following:

- The present price issue (on the development of self-employment)
- Blue jeans, disco, and other topics (on economic reform and the changes of aesthetic psychology)
- The development of modern culture in China
- Political education and interpersonal relationships
- Morality in modern culture
- The international economic situation
- Concepts of economic reform.

Book Reading and Review. The library not only lends books but also provides reading guidance, carries out book reviews, and directs radio and TV classes for junior and senior middle school teacher training. The number of people utilizing the library is 700,000. Five reading assistance lectures were delivered by famous authors and writers, with total audiences of 2,000. More than 400 participants were involved in book reviewing, and more than 20 articles were published.

Hobby Activities. These include many activities, some of which are detailed below.

Lantern Puzzle and Intelligence Contests. Eleven meetings probing the lantern puzzle theory and techniques were held, with thirty participants each time. Ninety-two lantern puzzle parties were held, with 20,000 persons participating. On Spring Festival, Lantern Festival, Mid-

Autumn, and other holidays, the Cultural Palace, along with the Shanghai TV Station and the Laodong and Wenhui newspapers, cosponsored the Family Lantern Puzzle Competition, the Happy Spring Festival Intelligence Competition, and other such activities. The competitors were the TV watchers, newspaper readers throughout the Jiangsu and Zhejiang provinces, and the Shanghai economic community.

Opera Singing. This is held in the Popular Art Hall on the second floor of the Cultural Palace. Every week there are two opportunities each for Beijing, Yue, and Hu opera singing, so that the residents, retired workers, and opera fans can entertain themselves with their own singing and performances. On rehearsal days, fans come from all parts of the city to satisfy their cravings for the opera. During 1986 these participants gave 200 performances of various operas. Over 30,000 people attended these performances.

Stamp Collecting. In the Stamp Collector Association, there is a membership of more than 10,000 people. During the Spring Festival, the seventh show of a Hundred Collector's Stamps for the Coming Spring was organized, and more than 50,000 persons attended. Sixteen stamp collecting lectures were delivered to an audience of 4,000 persons. A research group of 40 people scheduled activities each month studying stamp appraisal. Now the group is working on a Yearbook of Shanghai Stamp Collection.

Fishing. There is also an association of amateur anglers, which has a membership of 19,000 people. The association has held five seminars on the techniques of fishing, with over 1,500 participants, and a course of fishing referee training, with 100 referees completing the course. Five fishing competitions were held, with about 500 competitors.

Chess and Card Playing. Ten secondary Chinese chess training classes have been held, with 60 participants each. The Fifth Intelligence Bridge Cup Competition was held at the end of 1986. Ninety bridge teams made up of 600 competitors took part in the competition.

Literature Writing Course. This course is divided into song, poem, novel, drama, cross-talk (a type of humorous folk art), and other writing groups. The participants are all adult amateur writers, and their productions are either used as plays to be performed by the artists troupe, published in the *Constructor*, (the Cultural Palace quarterly), or made into TV films.

Art Training Courses. These courses are provided twice a year and have the purposes of cultivating active artistic cadres for grass-roots enterprises, teaching participant artists skills, and providing the Cultural Palace with outstanding graduates from the training classes. The number of classes are based on demand and programs offered have been
- Calligraphy, carving, and painting courses
- Yue and Hu opera singing courses

- Drama performing courses
- A folk music course
- Chorus singing classes
- Dancing training courses
- A wind instrument training course.

Performing Artists and Musicians. Shanghai Worker's Spare-Time Troupe of Artists and Musicians is the performing troupe of the Cultural Palace. Composed of more than 800 members from factories, schools, units, and other agencies, its repertoire includes brass music, folk music, orchestra, chorus, dancing, drama, opera, cross-talk shows, and circus. Performers give performances at the Cultural Palace in their spare time or during holidays. In recent years, the Jazming Performing Team of the troupe has been invited to Hong Kong, Japan, France, Italy, and other countries.

Since the troupe is a relatively high-ranked unit in Shanghai, it takes a leading role among other popular cultural and artistic units in Shanghai and helps organize large-scale activities.

During 1986 the troupe gave 426 performances, attended by 255,050 people. Among these performances were

- 88 performances of Pingtan singing
- 136 performances of cross-talk
- 26 plays of Beijing operas
- 80 performances of Yue operas
- 33 performances of Hu operas
- 3 dramas
- 46 brass band music concerts
- 41 light music concerts
- 45 folk music concerts.

Sports Competitions. The Cultural Palace does not have its own sports field, but it organizes and mobilizes sports activities of all workers in Shanghai. In 1986, 16 teams of 250 members were organized to take part in the Eighth Shanghai Sports Meeting, which included

- 1,200 teams participating in the Forth Worker's Basketball Cup Competition
- 56 teams participating in the Shanghai Worker's Class A and Class B Pingpong Competition
- 37 teams participating in the Tug-of-War Competition
- 400 members competing in the Shanghai Worker's Swimming Competition.

A system of professional conferences of worker's sports field directors and sports cadres has also been established.

Summary. As a workers' school and "a garden of happiness" for thirty years, the Shanghai Worker's Cultural Palace has attracted thousands of adults from various parts of the city to participate in all types of popular cultural activities. Most participants have increased their understanding and developed their competencies (which sometimes led them to a change of career).

Social educational activities are likely to lead to social effects. All the activities organized by the Shanghai Worker's Cultural Palace, such as lecture series, amateur groups, art training courses, performances, and sports activities, have enriched workers' lives, raised their cultural qualifications, deepened their appreciation of society and life, filled the gap of understanding between people, and strengthened social stability and unity. This is one of the great achievements in the field of adult social education.

Zhu Yuancheng is deputy director of the Shanghai Worker's Cultural Palace.

In China the problems of the handicapped are seen as society's problems. Modest gains have been made, but much more needs to be done.

Special Adult Education

Zhang Wanbing, Wang Xiaolai, Li Lei

Background

In China today there are approximately 20 million physically handicapped people. The social status of the handicapped is gradually rising as the socialist economy becomes more robust and prosperous. With government attention and support from society, most handicapped adults have found jobs and are making a contribution to society.

The education rights of the handicapped in China are protected by law. The Thirty-Ninth Amendment of the Constitution of China says that "the state develops the socialist cause of education in order to increase the nation's scientific and cultural level." The Forty-Fourth Amendment stipulates that "the state and society shall help the blind, deaf, and other handicapped citizens in the arrangement of their work, living, and education." In 1985 in the Decision on the Reformation of the Education System, the Central Committee of the CCP and the State Council decided to develop special education programs for visually and hearing impaired and mentally retarded children. In the Compulsory Education Act of the People's Republic of China it is further stipulated that local government at all levels should set up special educational classes for the visually and hearing impaired, physically disabled, and mentally retarded children.

In early 1985 the State Commission on Education, the National

Planning Committee, the Department of Labor, and the Department of Civil Affairs jointly set forth The Circular of Admission and Graduate Placement of the Handicapped Youth in Higher Education Institutions. This circular demands that all full-time universities and colleges provide equal treatment for physically disabled youth who can take care of themselves while pursuing their studies. After graduation, these individuals should be assigned a job by the state, as are other college graduates. If there is any difficulty in placement, the Civil Affairs Administration takes responsibility for assigning jobs.

According to this circular, as of the end of 1985 there were about 1,100 handicapped young people studying in China's colleges and universities. In 1985 Zhejiang University enrolled 8 handicapped people, and Hangzhou University enrolled 13. During 1984 and 1985, 41 handicapped people were admitted by Shanghai universities.

Education of the Handicapped

Special education in China is an indispensable part of socialist education and has been developing rapidly. Now it is gradually forming special independent units within primary, secondary, higher, and vocational technical education. All education activities, including special education, are carried out under the leadership of the Commission of Education and educational divisions in local governments. At the same time, since most adults with handicapping conditions are assigned to social welfare units in the civil administration, the civil affairs administration gives the education of the handicapped high priority. The Chinese Welfare Foundation for the Handicapped, the Chinese Association of the Blind and Deaf, and other national organizations also contribute to the education of the handicapped.

Education of the handicapped is based on different features of each group. The goal of education for the physically disabled is that they have the same opportunity for education as the able bodied, with the aim that the handicapped learn to take care of themselves.

Handicapped Student Association. At Yunnan University, a handicapped student's association was formed to facilitate understanding between handicapped and nonhandicapped students. The association is concerned with the needs and hopes of handicapped youth, helps them in self-study, and advocates that they be self-confident, self-reliant, and self-respecting. In 1986 the association proposed that other similar associations throughout the country be established.

Self-Study Examinations. The government and society also encourage the handicapped to receive higher education through TV universities, correspondence universities, and self-study examinations. In 1981 the self-study examination system was established, and it provides favorable opportunities for the handicapped in higher education. According to a 1985 rough survey of 19 provinces, municipalities directly under the central government, and autonomous regions, there were more than 400 handicapped people who took the self-study examination and received completion certificates for more than one university course.

In Beijing, Shanghai, and Tianjin, there were 10 handicapped examinees who passed all the required courses, and each received a university graduate diploma in either Chinese language and literature, mathematics, or English. In late 1982 the Shanghai Institute of Education started its program of self-study examination. Since then, nearly 200 handicapped people have applied to take examinations in majors such as Chinese language and English. The faculty and staff in the office of self-study examination assist handicapped participants by helping them buy textbooks and reading materials, giving them priority in the registration process, keeping in touch with them throughout their studies, and introducing relevant information for the hearing impaired.

The Chinese Welfare Foundation. With the support of the Beijing Broadcast and TV University, the Chinese Welfare Foundation for the Handicapped has set up classes to assist and guide hearing impaired participants enrolled in broadcast and TV universities. The foundation has accepted eighty handicapped young people to participate in broadcast and TV university study. In early 1986, along with the Central Committee of the Chinese National Party's Revolutionary Committee, the foundation set up the Zhongshan Institute to provide TV university classes to help self-study examination participants.

In China more and more local universities and colleges have begun to open their doors to handicapped youth. For example, the Shantong Binzhou Technical Institute has established a second medical treatment department especially for handicapped students, and the Jilin Fine Art Institution will also conduct courses in arts and crafts and folk music for students with handicaps.

The Chinese Welfare Foundation will also establish a Chinese Education Center for the Handicapped, which will administer vocational programs, preparatory programs, two- and three-year college programs, and university undergraduate programs. The center will serve as a training center for cadres engaged in work with the handicapped and will also provide opportunities for those with serious handicapping conditions who are not accepted by general universities.

To encourage the handicapped to rely on their own efforts, the foundation, together with the State Commission on Education and the Department of Civil Administration, has set up an award system for those learning through self-study as well as teacher awards in special education.

The Shanghai Association of the Blind and Deaf. Education for the hearing impaired is an important part of adult education for the handicapped. A sizeable proportion of handicapped people work in welfare production units (sheltered workshops) under the Civil Administration Office. In Shanghai, of 8,500 workers working in the welfare production units attached to the Civil Administration Bureau, 3,500 are hearing impaired. There are about 3,800 handicapped workers engaged in other professional jobs. The majority of these workers are illiterate owing to the lack of education during the Cultural Revolution combined with their physical limitations. Of the 24,000 handicapped people in Shanghai, 10,000 are blind and 14,000 are hearing impaired. The problem of unemployment for 10,000 handicapped people in urban areas still needs to be solved. The plan is to direct the handicapped to city welfare systems and to district and neighborhood sheltered workshops.

The Shanghai Association of the Blind and Deaf is an organization with branches in each district in Shanghai and associate units at the grass-roots level in factories, where most handicapped people are employed. This education network consists of citywide associations, associations in districts, and grass-roots associations. The grass-roots associations together with the educational divisions in factories provide literacy education for the handicapped. With support from the educational division, the special education associations in the districts have begun to run preparatory classes for middle school and remediation.

The Shanghai Association of the Blind and Deaf has an education division that focuses on junior and senior middle school education and vocational training. With help from the Department of Education, the association established a Shanghai Worker Spare-Time Vocational School for the handicapped. There are now twelve junior middle school education classes, with 216 students, 40 of whom have finished all the required courses and have received completion certificates. In 1985 the association also established worker spare-time senior middle school classes for the handicapped of Shanghai.

Between 1983 and 1985, the city developed eleven literacy tests, seven of which are for the visually impaired, four of which are for the hearing impaired. From 1983 to 1985, five centralized examinations at the junior middle school level were organized, two for the visually impaired, and three for the hearing impaired.

Out of 3,146 handicapped workers in 3 districts, 205 have become literate and 1,535 have reached senior elementary school level; 1,241 have reached junior middle school level; 145 have reached senior middle school level; and 20 are now enrolled in higher education.

Vocational Education. Currently, vocational technical education for the handicapped is making steady progress throughout the country. In the last three years in Shanghai, more than 40 technical training classes have been provided, and 1,000 handicapped people have received training in designing, sewing, knitting, drawing, woodworking, massage, and acupuncture. With help from the Shanghai Artists Association, the Shanghai Association of the Handicapped started a three-month seminar for technical drawing training. Each seminar enrolls about 20 students. The applicants consist of the hearing impaired who are engaged in artistic work in enterprises. All students take an entrance examination before they are admitted. The teaching staff are well-known artists and instructors from the China Painting Institute.

The Shenyang Kangfu Professional School is a vocational school for the handicapped that was organized three years ago by the Shenyang Association of Handicapped Youth. The emergence of that school depended on the support the school received from governmental units and all the social organizations in the city of Shenyang. Some of the facilities are donated by army units and factories, and some were bought at favorable prices directly from factories. The teaching staff are volunteers who request minimal financial support. Many contribute donations to the school. In just three years the school has provided five seminars on vocational training, including seminars on electric equipment repairing, acupuncture and massage, arts and crafts, tailoring and sewing, watch and clock repairing, and general theory of Chinese medicine. Altogether, the school has trained 1,000 handicapped people and about 600 participants have received jobs. In China, the problems of the handicapped are a social problem. Modest gains have been made; much now needs to be done.

Zhang Wanbing is chair of the Department of Education, Shanghai Civil Administration Bureau. Wang Xiaolai and Li Lei are cadres of the Department of Education, Shanghai Civil Administration Bureau.

Part 2.

Types of Provision

Adult schools have different missions: general studies and scientific knowledge, professional technology, or art and cultural life.

Adult Institutional Provision

Fang Jing, Gao Zhuomin

Background

Adult institutional education refers to schools that provide learning opportunities for adults. These educational institutions provide purposeful, organized, and systematic activities. Activities conducted in adult schools are classified as adult institutional education.

Schools for adults appeared in China in the early twentieth century. Between 1930 and 1940, adult schools developed quickly in some industrial cities. In the 1940s Shanghai had 400 mass and remedial schools. Among these were the Chinese vocational remedial schools founded by Huang Yanpei, the Lixing Accounting School founded by Pen Xuluen, and the experimental mass schools founded by Yu Qingtang. These schools greatly contributed to the promotion of adult educational level, technical skills, and adult employment opportunities.

Adult Education in Shanghai

Adult education developed faster in China's urban areas than in rural areas, and adult education in Shanghai has developed the fastest in China in size and number of schools and teaching staff. One out of ten adult learners in higher educational adult institutions in China is in Shanghai, and in 1950 over 1.33 million were enrolled in adult schools. Accordingly, the Shanghai experience is highlighted in this chapter.

In general, adult schools in the urban areas operate in the following manner: First, adult schools are run by the government, research institutions, full-time day schools, and social organizations. There are also a few private adult schools. Second, adult schools have different missions. They either focus on general studies and scientific knowledge, adult professional technology, or on art and cultural education.

At present, there are almost no adult elementary schools in Shanghai. Those in existence are attached to adult secondary schools. In Shanghai there are mainly adult secondary schools and adult higher schools.

The ratio of students receiving secondary education to those receiving higher education is nine to one. Adult school education is mainly conducted in adults' spare time, but some learners, with their working units' permission, spend some of their production and working hours studying.

Adult education classes in Shanghai for the most part use a lecture format. Each school invites scholars and professors to give lectures, and some also invite skilled workers with teaching experience to help students.

Adult schools have full-time staff and full-time and part-time instructors. Only a few schools have several full-time administrators, and all teaching is conducted by invited part-time instructors. At present, there are 10,000 professional faculties and staff in the Shanghai adult secondary schools. Apart from teaching, full-time instructors are responsible for the curriculum and for helping part-time instructors. In general, adult schools, whose objectives are divided into general studies and scientific knowledge studies, invite instructors from full-time schools and retired teachers to teach. Secondary vocational schools select technicians and administrators from enterprises as teachers.

Most adult schools receive funds from different sources. Schools are responsible for fund raising in addition to charging tuition. Funds for adult schools operated by the government and its educational department or by an enterprise are guaranteed, but some schools attempt to raise additional funds to improve their teaching conditions.

Tuition fees vary from school to school. In general, the tuition for adult secondary schools is usually less than 100 yuan, and tuition for adult higher educational schools is only 300 to 400 yuan. In a few adult higher educational schools, fees for some educational activities are relatively high (approximately 1,000 yuan a year) and are paid by the working unit, if permission to study has been granted. The student also receives full pay while studying. Very few adult students pay their own tuition.

Adult schools are nonprofit institutions. Most of their money is spent on regular educational activities under the supervision of relevant financial divisions. If a school needs to set up school buildings or purchase additional teaching facilities, a budget is submitted to the unit responsible for reviewing and approving the funds.

The textbooks for adult schools are edited by the government education department. Textbooks used by full-time schools are used if the adult school does not have comparable books. Sometimes schools also develop their own textbooks and teaching materials. These materials are revised after they have been used in class for some time.

After finishing their studies in adult schools, students are issued diplomas according to their areas of study. Presently, government-accredited schools issue secondary education, secondary technical education, and higher education graduate diplomas. Most adult schools issue two- or three-year college diplomas. A few schools issue four-year university diplomas. Very few schools award bachelor degrees. Until recently, only adult educational institutions attached to full-time colleges and universities had the right to award master's degrees.

Adult schools also award single-course certificates. Those who have finished vocational or technical training are awarded job certificates. Even those who study art, literature, physical education, and recreation only for leisure are awarded relevant certificates. Diplomas and certificates issued by accredited schools or the government are of great significance to society.

Any adult wanting a diploma or a vocational and technical certificate must take certain examinations. Enrollment for most secondary schools occurs twice a year, but adult higher educational schools recruit students only once a year. Recently, joint admissions were adopted, dates, and content of standardized examinations were jointly determined, and standardized criteria for reviewing and scoring examinations were developed. Schools taking part in joint admission select the best examinees. Preparatory seminars to help adults pass the entrance examinations are often held. After registration, each school makes a list of the students who intend to obtain a certificate on completion of their studies. A list is given to the departments responsible for maintaining student records. In China, any student studying for a diploma or certificate must take an examination organized and prepared by the government. If the examination is passed, a diploma or certificate is issued. Students can ask for a leave from their working units to prepare for the examinations. Generally, working units will allow several days off for exam preparation.

In the late 1970s Shanghai did not have enough adult schools. Only one or two out of three to five adults who passed the entrance examinations had a chance for admission. The development of adult schools in recent years has enabled many adults to attend schools. The problem now for some adult schools in Shanghai is how to meet new societal needs. In response, adult schools are becoming more flexible in terms of teaching content and ways of organizing work.

The two levels of Shanghai government, the municipal and district (county) levels, have established adult schools in every district. Seven percent of all enterprises operate adult education programs. In recent years, there has been a decrease in adult schools that deliver general education programs, whereas there has been a gradual increase in schools that teach mainly vocational courses.

Adult higher educational schools appeared in the late 1950s in Shanghai; evening schools attached to full-time higher educational schools appeared in the 1940s. In the late 1970s, adult higher educational institutions developed relatively fast, and currently there are sixty adult higher educational institutions operated by enterprises and by the educational departments of the municipal and district governments.

Among these higher educational institutions, the Shanghai Second University of Industry (SSUI) is the largest comprehensive adult university. It was founded in 1960 and focuses on engineering, with management and humanities as minors. As a comprehensive university, it has ten departments located in ten geographical divisions. There are presently 1,103 faculty members and staff and 7,966 students. In the 26 years since its founding, SSUI has trained 35,000 talented people, 5,000 of whom are three-year college program graduates and four-year university program graduates who are working in more than 2,000 factories and enterprises.

To give the reader a clearer picture of China's adult school education, four adult institutions will be discussed.

Shanghai Changning District First Spare-Time Secondary School.
In the early 1950s there were more than 10 similar district adult secondary schools in Shanghai. By 1958 there were 51 similar schools, with an enrollment of 60,000 students. These schools were located in industrial, commercial, and residential areas so that citizens and workers would be within walking distance. These schools were an indispensable element in enterprise worker's education and were administered by the educational departments of district governments. In 1985 there were 58 such schools.

Changning District First Spare-Time Secondary School was founded in 1957. The school has 35 full-time faculty and staff and 23 part-time instructors. Forty percent of the students are enrolled in junior courses. In 1986 junior courses were cancelled, because there were fewer and fewer people who took these courses. Now the school is a senior high school, providing only senior general programs. In 1986 there were 778 students in science classes, 823 students in humanities classes, and 398 students in remedial classes.

According to the stipulations of the Shanghai Municipal Education Bureau, adults in senior science as well as humanities courses should take five subjects such as Chinese, politics, mathematics, physics, and chemistry. Both science and humanities courses require 900 class hours. Students can, according to their own schedule, select one or two courses each semester. Every time a course finishes, students take a standardized examination relevant to the course. The questions and content of the examination are based on the teaching outline from the Municipal Education Bureau. When students pass one course, they are awarded completion certificates. When students have received five completion certificates, they can be awarded a senior high school graduate diploma, which is validated and officially sealed by the district Education Bureau. This diploma is recognized by the government, and some foreign consulates in Shanghai also recognize this diploma when issuing a visa for study abroad.

Senior high school review classes exist for those adults who want to study in higher educational institutions. After a period of working, some adults may forget what they have learned in senior high schools and hope that a systematic review will help them pass the national higher education entrance examination. No entrance examination is required for adults who wish to participate in the review classes. According to a general survey, 700 graduates from the science and humanities review classes have been admitted into several higher educational institutions, most of which are adult higher educational schools.

Changning District Worker Secondary Technical School. This school began to develop into a large school only several years ago. In 1986 there were 12 similar schools in Shanghai, with 30,000 students. Founded in 1956, the Changning Worker Secondary Technical School is an educational institution with various functions. Formerly it was a district cadre spare-time education school. In 1984, with the government's approval, it took its present form. In 1986 this school provided political work, industrial enterprise, management, electronic, and chemical engineering for 391 participants. The school has thirty-five full-time teachers and forty staff. Most teachers have graduated from teachers' colleges or normal universities.

The school has set up TV secondary technical school stations, and 13 study classes were offered in several enterprises throughout the district for 426 participants, including a self-study assistant class for 41 secondary law majors, which was opened in association with the district Judicial Bureau, and a senior Chinese review class, which opened with 450 students.

The school is responsible for training enterprise leaders throughout the district. Each training session is offered for five weeks to full-time students, and each seminar has thirty participants.

Adult students who want to obtain a secondary technical school graduate diploma take an entrance examination. The examination for secondary technical schools in Shanghai is organized by the municipal Education Bureau. A diploma for an engineering major requires 2,100 class hours and for a humanities major, 1,800 hours.

Shanghai Foreign Trade Worker University. Approved by the Shanghai municipal government in 1980 and put on the record of the State Commission of Education, the Shanghai Foreign Trade Worker University is an adult higher educational institution run by the municipal Foreign Trade Bureau. The university is open only to the workers in the Shanghai foreign trade system and is the source of higher education in the system. The university currently has 1,200 students. One-fourth of the more than 1,000 students in the university are females. The age range of students is between nineteen and thirty-nine, with an average age of twenty-seven. Students usually have two years of work experience, and most are engaged in foreign trade. There are 210 faculty and staff members, of whom 98 are teachers.

The university offers courses in foreign economics, English for trade, management, transportation and foreign trade, finance, and accounting. Apart from higher educational programs, the university has opened five courses in secondary technical education, which include foreign trade, documents and files, statistics, finance and accounting, and storage and transportation. The university also provides short-term seminars and senior high school review courses. In addition, the university helps provide assistant work for the Shanghai TV University.

Beginning in 1984 the Shanghai Foreign Trade Worker University was opened to all in the country. Workers from ten provinces and cities applied for admission. Adult students either major in foreign trade or management. The university prefers applicants with basic knowledge of a foreign language and some work experience. In addition to providing pertinent records, students must take the standardized entrance examination before being accepted to the university.

The period of schooling for the junior college program is three years. The program has five specialities, which are designed according to the teaching outline for full-time students in higher education. The adult learning styles are taken into account. Generally, each speciality requires more than ten courses. Five specialities are combined with thirty different courses, including philosophy, Chinese, mathematics, computer science, English and basic trade English, economics, commercial morality, introduction to foreign trade, finance, foreign trade planning, foreign trade transportation, import and export business, marketing, international finance, and international commercial laws.

Secondary professional study in the university requires two years in five specialities with approximately twenty courses. The courses include philosophy, Chinese, mathematics, computer science, economics, import and export, foreign trade statistics, foreign trade accounting, foreign trade file and records, and foreign trade storage and transportation.

Before graduation, both graduates in the three-year college program and the two-year secondary technical program are required to pass all course examinations and to write a graduation thesis. (Graduates from the secondary technical program write graduate compositions.) Diplomas are issued by adult institutions, and society treats diplomas like those issued by full-time institutions.

The Luwan District Spare-Time University. There are twelve districts in the Shanghai urban area, eleven of which have opened district spare-time universities. These universities are district adult higher educational institutions. Early in 1958 there were five of these institutions in Shanghai; approval was obtained from the municipal government and filed with the central government, and institutions were operated by local district governments.

The primary function of these institutions is to serve medium- and small-scale enterprises in local districts. Eleven spare-time universities jointly recruit students from the city, enabling students to attend schools in their residential vicinity. In 1985 district spare-time universities had 26,464 students, including 15,180 students in three-year college programs, 6,949 students in single-course programs, and 433 participants in various kinds of seminars. There were altogether 1,690 faculty and staff members, including 1,108 full-time teachers.

The Luwan District Spare-Time University was founded in 1960. In 1986 the university provided eight specialities: Chinese language and literature, secretarial work, light industrial mechanics, electronic automation, computer science, foreign trade economics, enterprise business, and management and administration. These specialities are part of the three-year college program. The university is very much concerned about new developments in applied scientific technology and often provides relevant courses in these areas. In 1986 the university had 1,744 adult students in such courses. Since the founding of the university, there have been 1,190 graduates from three-year college programs, and 13,601 single-course completion certificates have been issued. The university has 200 faculty and staff members, including 136 teachers.

The three teaching divisions of the university are foundations, engineering, and humanities. The university also offers courses in teaching, general affairs, training, and scientific research. The university has set up a working station for the Shanghai TV University.

The Luwan District Spare-Time University has served thousands of professional experts. Some graduates often come to the university to refresh their knowledge and take new courses. Some graduates have received national or Shanghai municipal awards for their innovations.

Fang Jing is a member of the Shanghai Association of Philosophy and Social Sciences, and secretary general of the Shanghai Adult Education Research Society.

Gao Zhuomin is director of District Adult Education Research Society.

By 1985 300 universities provided correspondence education, and 400 universities established evening colleges; approximately 5 million participants were enrolled, which amounts to 28 percent of the full-time traditional university students.

University Adult Provision

Lin Houxiang, Zhang Yi

Background

Many universities in China, including the leading ones, provide adult education programs. Correspondence education and evening college education are important components of China's higher education and an inseparable part of China's general education system.

Early in the year following the birth of New China, evening colleges began to emerge, followed by correspondence education. In 1965 there were 123 universities that offered correspondence education, and 83 universities established evening colleges. There were 150,000 participants in correspondence programs and evening colleges—22 percent of all full-time students. There were 138 specialities offered, such as industry, agriculture, language, science, forestry, medicine, teacher training, finance, law, and physical education.

The development of adult education in universities owes its existence to government policy. The State Higher Education Department not only directed the development of general higher education but also paid great attention to adult higher education. Rules and regulations were developed by the department to support adult education programs in universities. Any university that intended to provide adult education had to be ratified by the department, and only those with sufficient resources were allowed to establish programs. Instructional outlines, objectives and purposes, period of study, content offered, and teaching plans of correspondence education and evening colleges were required to be consistent with the regulations stipulated by the department. This development ended with the Cultural Revolution.

In the late 1970s, the Ten Year Chaos ended. The era of economic development required a great number of scientists and technicians. Universities felt the pressure, for they were neither able to meet the demand for more talented individuals nor to address the desire of workers for higher education. Correspondence education and evening colleges were quickly restored. The government strongly supported adult education programs in universities, recognizing that this was the only way to lessen the pressure on general higher education.

In September 1980 the State Council ratified the Decision on Large-Scale Development of Correspondence Education and Evening College in Universities proposed by the State Education Department. This document points out that adult education in universities is an economical and efficient means of raising the nation's education level. Adult education programs were to become an inseparable part of general higher education. The department also convened several national conferences and developed a series of policies and regulations. Adult education programs should, as the policies stated, be formalized and quality controlled. The government recognized the educational level of graduates from correspondence education and evening colleges. Wages and benefits received by these graduates were to be the same as those of graduates from traditional university and college programs.

These policies and regulations gave the development of adult education in universities momentum and encouraged high enrollment. By 1985 300 universities provided correspondence education, and 400 universities established evening colleges. Participants reached 4.9 million—28 percent of the full-time university students. Since the founding of the People's Republic of China, 200,000 individuals have graduated from correspondence education programs and evening colleges.

Correspondence Higher Education in Universities

Since 1980 correspondence higher education in universities has been included in the development plan of state education. Only those universities who have sufficient resources, strong leadership, and quality programs are allowed to provide correspondence education service. Universities that desire to offer correspondence education programs must submit an application to the State Education Department and obtain ratification prior to initiation. In this way the quality of correspondence education can be guaranteed at least in respect to the capacity of the university.

Program Planning. Program planning, fundamental to institutional activities, must take the department's regulations into consideration. These regulations include the following:

1. Participants must be workers and peasants. The length of schooling of undergraduate equivalent courses is five to six years.

2. Programs must be equivalent to the traditional undergraduate curriculum to ensure the participants a university-level education.

3. Content should be concise, focusing on basic theory; presentation should begin from the simple and move to the complex.

4. The courses offered and the hours of instruction of foundation courses and major courses must be the same as those for regular undergraduates. Electives such as politics and physical education are not required.

5. Instruction and learning (including independent learning) should be no less than a total of 5,500 hours. Taking into account the practical considerations of the participants, the number of instruction hours a week should not exceed 18.

Admission Requirements. To make effective use of what is learned from correspondence education, participants, who must have a secondary education, are asked to enroll in specialities that have close relationship to their present jobs. The age limit for applicants is forty, permission must be obtained from the working unit, and the entrance examination must be passed before an applicant can be admitted. Before 1985 examination papers were required by universities that offered correspondence education. To ensure the quality of these papers and hence of those admitted, the State Education Department decided that starting in 1985, entrance examinations must be standardized and that a statewide entrance examination would take place each year. Admissions offices of adult higher education were established in those provinces with responsibility for administering admission tests. Two years of working experience is also required for admission in some universities. Participants are usually recruited from cities and neighboring provinces. The State Education Department is sometimes involved in the adjustment of course offerings and recruitment areas.

Textbooks. There are two types of textbooks: One is compiled by correspondence teachers; the other is similar to books used by traditional university students. In compiling textbooks, teachers take full account of both the characteristics of independent learning and the demands of the program outline. These textbooks are usually detailed and easy to read. Exercises, simulation, examination, and independent study methods are included in textbooks. When using textbooks borrowed from universities, auxiliary learning materials and independent study methods are provided by the teachers.

Method of Instruction. The main method in correspondence edu-

cation is independent study. Face-to-face instruction is a supplementary measure. The main educational process includes
- Compilation of teaching and auxiliary materials
- Advisement during independent study
- Correction of homework
- Face-to-face instruction and answering of questions
- Intensive direction of reviews, examinations, and experiments at the end of each semester
- Direction and organization of a thesis and graduate research.

Correspondence Education Stations. An important role is played by correspondence education stations, which cover a wide geographical area. Since most participants live far from the universities offering correspondence education programs, these stations take on part of the tasks of the universities to help participants in their vicinities. Correspondence stations are established with the cooperation of the universities and local technical organizations or enterprises. These units hope that the university will admit their participants and train them for more responsible positions. The universities agree to train these employees, and in return, units must establish and fund correspondence stations.

Some correspondence stations are established in local colleges or universities. Funds for these stations come from two sources: (1) tuition provided by the units that send their employees and (2) the local government.

The main task of correspondence stations is to invite teachers from local communities to organize face-to-face instruction and other auxiliary teaching methods according to the program plans of the correspondence offices. The stations also organize reviews and conduct experiments and examinations. Part-time teachers are required to have a higher education and teaching experience. Correspondence offices can inspect the qualifications of the invited teachers and dismiss them if they do not meet the requirements.

Funding. Funds are essential in conducting correspondence education. Before 1985 funds came from the state budget and were allocated to the university at the rate of 100 yuan per participant. Beginning in 1985 only correspondence education programs offered by teacher preparation universities or colleges were eligible to receive state funds. Otherwise, programs had to obtain funds through tuition obtained from the units that sent the employee. Tuition costs are regulated at 170 yuan per participant enrolled in science and technology, and 120 yuan per participant enrolled in liberal arts. Tuition is paid by the working units, and participants only pay for their textbooks, teaching materials, and postage. Working units also provide paid educational leave.

Tongji University. Universities place great emphasis on the quality of correspondence education. People are accustomed to the way universities train full-time students and often suspect the quality of spare-time education. Universities are striving to raise the quality of correspondence education to eliminate this bias. Through years of experience, some universities have emerged with high-quality correspondence education and enjoy a good reputation; Tongji University is one of these institutions.

Located in Shanghai, Tongji University, one of the leading comprehensive universities in China, prepares science and engineering professionals. One of the earliest institutions in China allowed to grant bachelor's degrees to engineering students, Tongji University has been engaged in correspondence education for thirty years and has 150 correspondence teachers, 60 percent of whom are full-time.

Students at Tongji University must take three to four courses each semester and hand in homework three to six times a semester. Participants who do not finish two-thirds of the homework are not eligible to take the examinations. The college asks teachers to emphasize independent study methods. Written questions submitted by participants must be addressed within three days by the teachers. The college also emphasizes the importance of compiling teaching materials, including films and videotapes. The college gives serious attention to examinations, especially to the quality of papers and the rigor of examinations. Eighty percent of the university's participants graduate.

Summary. Correspondence education costs about one-fourth to one-third less than general education and is designed to address the needs of production. Since funds are limited, correspondence education is quickly becoming an important part of the country's educational program. With the advent of modern instructional technologies such as tape recording, video films, and TV technology, correspondence education will play an important role in the training of talented people.

University Evening Colleges

The evening college is another form of university adult education, one whose scale and extent is smaller than correspondence education.

Evening colleges have been established in approximately 50 percent of the universities in China. The number of universities offering evening college programs is larger than the number offering correspondence education. One reason for this difference is that the administration and instruction processes of evening colleges are similar to those of regular universities. However, the scale and extent of evening colleges are restricted by factors such as the number of teachers available, teaching facilities, and areas of recruitment.

As with correspondence education, the state encourages universities to conduct evening colleges. However, universities that intend to do so must submit applications and be approved. Participants are admitted through standardized entrance examinations in adult higher education.

Since education in evening colleges is conducted mainly through face-to-face instruction, participants should attend no less than ten hours per week. Fifty percent of the courses are offered in the evenings.

To those who graduate from secondary technical schools, evening college is a means of pursuing a higher education. The state grants that evening colleges can have their own full-time teachers and are entitled to ask the working units that send participants to pay tuition of 350 yuan per participant per year. In order to encourage universities to open night colleges, local governments in some provinces allocate part of their local budget to the universities. For example, the Shanghai municipal government allocates 100 to 200 yuan per participant each year to the universities that admit participants to evening colleges from Shanghai.

The period of study in evening colleges is usually five and a half years. Instruction outlines and requirements are similar to those of traditional universities. Politics and physical education are not offered. Instructional hours total 2,200. There are two semesters per year, and there are over 200 hours in one semester. Instruction is usually arranged four times a week, twice in the evening and two afternoons a week. The two half days are actually working days. Just as in correspondence education, the state stipulates that an evening college participant can have one day paid leave per week for study and one to two weeks paid leave at the end of semesters for review and examinations. The state fully recognizes evening college education, and graduates are eligible to have the same allotment as traditional university graduates.

Unlike correspondence education, which requires a stable team of full-time teachers, most teachers in evening colleges are part-time. Usually they are full-time university teachers who do extra assignments for extra pay. The learning conditions in evening colleges are better than those of correspondence education in that participants have more interactions with teachers and thus problems and questions can be addressed more directly. However, this does not mean that part-time study is easy. A participant has a twofold responsibility: one to the working unit and one to the college. Once a participant stops studies for a period of time, he or she will be dismissed. Some participants must pay tuition themselves. Working units do not pay the tuition in some cases, either because there are too many participants in the unit for the size of the education fund or because the leaders do not see the importance of adult education. A few leaders do not even allow their employees to participate for fear that participation might affect production. But most leaders of enterprises see education as a means of promoting production and thus encourage employees to participate.

Practice has demonstrated that evening college education is a means of fully employing the potential of a university and that the quality of the education can be guaranteed. It is bound to develop more fully.

Other Forms of Adult Education in Universities

In addition to degree programs, universities also provide other forms of adult education services. These include the auditing of courses by adults from enterprises and organizations; the training of inservice personnel based on contracts developed between the university and enterprises or organizations; and workshops and seminars. On completion of these activities, certificates are issued to the participants.

The auditing of courses by adult participants is a form widely used by universities in their adult education service. In this way participants, most of whom have already had some higher education, can update their knowledge in their own fields. Before each semester, all courses are announced. A small audit fee is required, which is usually paid by the working units. Textbooks are purchased by individual participants. The participants are allowed to take examinations at the end of a semester.

Participants in training based on contracts are usually technical managers. The contracts stipulate items such as the content, time limit, number of trainees universities should admit, and fees that enterprises or organizations shall provide. The time limit is settled according to the content to be covered. When the training is completed, certificates are granted. Workshops or seminars are provided to meet general needs. The content includes required subjects such as foreign languages, accounting, and technology. The period of time varies from several weeks to several months. Any individual who has foundational knowledge and is willing to pay fees is eligible to participate. A certificate is granted if the individual finishes the program and passes the examination.

Conclusion

China has the largest population in the world. To provide adult education services by using the full potential of the universities is an economical and practical measure. It can be predicted that along with economic construction, adult education in universities will expand greatly in the future.

Lin Houxiang is vice-president of the Correspondence College of Tongji University.

Zhang Yi is head of the Administrative Office of the Correspondence College of Tongji University.

Some enterprises consider continuing education planning as important as production construction planning.

Postuniversity Provision

Zhou Qinggong, He Jie

Postuniversity continuing education in China is a part of adult education. Though started at the founding of New China, it did not come into its own until the nation began to concentrate on economic construction.

Agencies for Continuing Education

Governmental Structuring of Schools. The ministries of the State Council provide continuing education for specialists. For example, the Ministry of Mechanical Building has established a Mechanical Engineer Refresher University with periodic instruction and self study as its main instructional approach. At present, it has about 10,000 students. The Ministry of the Coal Industry has established a Mechanization of Excavation Technology Study Center, which has gradually formed a comprehensive training base for advanced technicians and specialists. In the past few years, the center has trained about 200 bureau-level general engineers, 400 bureau-level engineers, and more than 500 assistant engineers and technicians. Heilongjiang province has established a Specialist Education Committee and has decided to establish a Technical Cadre Continuing Education College. In towns and cities within the province, colleges for continuing education are being established. Guangxi Zhaung autonomous region has allocated special funds for establishing the Gaungxi Science and Technology Education Center. Jilin Provincial

Health Sector has established 29 training bases responsible for the continuing education of doctors and nurses. In the past four years, it has trained 18,000 persons—18 percent of the total number of health cadres in the province.

Daqing has stipulated that training of technicians above the engineer level be organized by the municipality and assistant engineers and technicians be organized by the district government. Four training centers have been established to train an annual total of 1,000 specialists.

Schools Run by Industrial Enterprises. Industrial enterprises organize their own engineering and professional personnel for continuing education. The following are characteristics of continuing education run by industrial enterprises:

1. *Learning is associated with the needs of production and construction of the working units.* For example, Shanghai Oil-Chemical Engineering Plant has organized technicians to learn new skills and knowledge relevant to imported items and new technologies for the plant. A team of engineering technicians who have mastered new technologies has been formed and the process of productive construction guaranteed. Shenyang Heavy Machinery Plant requires adult learners to bring production problems to the study of new technologies. Since 1981 Baicheng City Machine Tool Plant has sent engineers to study in colleges and universities to develop the ability to design new products. The participants have now designed and made three types of advanced machine tools.

2. *Specialists are systematically trained.* Many enterprises sponsor a variety of continuing education classes for engineers and send specialists to formalized advanced study courses. Some enterprises encourage engineers and high-level engineers to study foreign languages in order to form a technical team prepared for importing new technologies. Shanghai General Oil-Chemical Engineering Plant has developed an overall plan for graduates for colleges and universities that includes internship training and continuing education.

3. *Steps are actively taken to guarantee the regularity of continuing education.* Some enterprises consider continuing education planning as important as production construction planning. Plans are developed by companies at the beginning of each year and then sent to each branch, workshop, section, and office for review. At the end of the year, these plans are re-examined. Some enterprises have developed criteria for the continuing education of engineers, specialists, and technicians. Rules of reward and punishment are stipulated. Participants' performance in learning will decide, to a certain degree, job promotion as well as fringe benefits.

Schools Run by Research Organizations and Higher Educational Institutions. The main content of specialist and teacher continuing education is remediation of basic theories within the professions and study of relevant new technologies, theories, and experimental technologies. In recent years, scientific research organizations and higher educational institutions have organized classes in foreign languages and computer science. In addition to training classes, academic exchange and exchange programs with other countries are used. Specialists and teachers improve their skills through writing books and thesis and by translating works. Systematic reading is also greatly emphasized. For instance, in 1984 one scientific research institution allocated 10,000 yuan (about 5,000 U.S. dollars) a year to send scientific specialists over 45 years of age to a retreat house for a "recuperating self-study class."

Continuing education for scientific specialists and teachers in higher education institutions has certain regulations that serve to integrate study with the learners' titles, positions, and salary promotions. The China Academy of Sciences, has issued Detailed Tentative Regulations on Inservice Personnel Application for Master's and Doctorate Degrees, which greatly encourage scientific specialists and teachers to pursue advanced study.

In addition to offering continuing education in their own working units, many scientific research organizations and higher educational institutions provide education for industrial and mineral enterprises and for the society in general. Qinghua University established a Department of Continuing Education in 1978 and has offered several training classes in continuing education. In 1985 the university formally established the College of Continuing Education. The Eastern China Chemical Engineering Institute, Northwestern Industry University, the Shanghai Second University of Industry, and the Harbing Ship Engineering Institute have also established colleges or departments of continuing education.

Programs Administered by Academic Associations, Democratic Parties, and Other Social Forces. In recent years, academic associations have restored or built eighty-six science and technology refresher colleges and universities throughout the country to provide engineers and specialists with continuing education. With local governmental support, the associations run their programs at different levels and in different ways. There have been 430,000 persons trained at these institutions over the last few years. Science and technology refresher colleges in Beijing, Shengyang, Wuhan, Dalian, and Liuzhou have become important bases of continuing education for local science and technology leaders.

The Chinese Science and Technology Association, together with 186 academic groups and provincial associations, has held many lectures, refresher classes, and workshops. About 1 million different specialists have participated in this type of continuing education. The Chinese Association of Agriculture has held a series of training classes on basic atomic energy applications to agriculture.

To coordinate and improve the quality of continuing education for specialists, the Chinese Association of Science and Technology has established a Continuing Education Task Committee, chaired by Liu Lanying, a member of the Chinese Academic Committee and vice-chair of the Chinese Science and Technology Association.

Chinese nongovernmental organizations such as democratic parties and alumni associations of some key universities have also established continuing education programs. The Chinese Worker and Peasant Democratic Party established the Qianjin Spare-Time School of Continuing Education in Shanghai. At present, funds for these institutions come mainly from donations and tuition. Very few schools can get appropriations from the government.

Apart from the programs offered by the above-mentioned groups, there are jointly sponsored programs through co-ops. For example, fifteen researcher teaching units and productive units in the southwest and northwest part of China have established a Southwestern and Northwestern Science Cooperation Center in cooperation with the Northwestern Polytechnical University. In the Guangxi Zhuang autonomous region, the Guilin City and Middle China Industry College in Wuhan have jointly established a Guilin Science and Teaching Center to conduct continuing education.

Types of Programs

The following are four types of programs in China's continuing education system.

Supplementary Programs. These types of programs include basic theory studies, computer skills classes, and foreign languages studies. Many units organize specialists to study linear algebra, mathematical physics equations, probability, and statistics. To keep up with the modern technological revolution, many units emphasize the importance of computer science.

Education for Career Change. This type of continuing education helps scientific specialists learn new skills and knowledge on changing their working posts. For example, in order to transfer some chemical engineer specialists to environmental protection posts, the Shanghai Municipal Environment Protection Bureau has asked spare-time science and technology institutes to open classes on environmental protection so that engineers can study environmental analysis and control, environmental quality assessment, sewage treatment, air pollution and protection, noise control and abatement, and other similar sciences.

New Technology Education. This type of education refers to courses that help specialists study new theories and technologies and examine new trends in the development of technology. For example, the Changchun Auto Research Institute has chosen courses such as limited unit, optimum design, reliable design, model analysis, fatigue life, computer aided design (CAD), and computer aided manufacture (CAM) for engineers. The Worker University of the Chinese Science Institute offers Sensor Technology and Test of Weak Signals, two short-term seminars attended by about 200 participants from all parts of the country.

Research Education. This is the highest level of continuing education in China. It facilitates the development of science and improves the skill of prominent figures in science. The Chinese Association of Automation has held an Engineering Control Project research class for high-level engineers from eighty colleges and universities. This class has helped advance automation science in China. The Number 33 Research Institute of the Ministry of Electronics Industry organized a reading group on magnetic storm technology, which lasted a year. Its target group was mainly engineers who participated in group discussions for half a day each week.

In practice, all units that operate schools, classes, or seminars are concerned about content in continuing education. Content should be useful and subject-matter oriented. Content is decided according to the needs of the local districts, economic units, and productive units as well as by teachers and researchers.

Basic Approaches of Continuing Education

Generally, there are five teaching approaches in continuing education in China.

Classroom Sessions. Institutions run classes (training classes, refresher classes, discussion classes) according to the content of the program. There are short- and long-term classes: Long-term classes last from three to four months or one to two years; short-term classes last only five to six days. The students are spare-time, part-time, or full-time. Some classes are held once or twice a week, while some are concentrated during specified times. At present, short-term classes are most commonly used to study one subject or issue. Some refresher classes are run by higher educational schools for engineers who study several subjects systematically. Instructors are usually specialists and scholars invited from colleges, universities, science and research institutions, enterprises, associations, or other agencies.

Lectures. Foreign experts and scholars are invited to give lectures and academic reports. Lectures are one of the basic methods of organizing people to study new technologies, theories, and the latest scientific developments and trends.

Research agencies and higher educational institutions always use the lecture approach. In 1984 the China Academy of Sciences offered almost 100 lectures, with approximately 10,000 participants. In recent years the Wugong Agricultural Research Center of Shanxi province has invited more than 30 foreign experts from the United States, Japan, Germany, and Australia to give 62 lectures, with more than 2,000 people in attendance.

Academic Exchange. In this approach, which has been adopted by most units, specialists participate in a variety of academic exchanges to broaden their knowledge base.

Since 1980 the Daqing Oil Administration Bureau, for example, has sent 200 specialists to take part in international oil engineering technology conferences. The Tianjin Engineering Investigation and Design Institute has sent 10 persons abroad to exchange technologies with foreign countries and to discuss and import advanced technologies and experiences.

Professional Science and other affiliated associations are the main organizations that carry out exchange programs. Under the Shanghai Association of Science 25 associations held 1,350 academic meetings, with an audience of 737,000.

Self-Study, Correspondence, and TV Education. Self-study in China is an important approach in continuing education. Many units have drawn up a full curriculum and examination system for scientific specialists and technicians to promote their continuing education, and participants are asked to make study plans according to requirements and to take examinations regularly in order to enhance and augment their self-studies. Correspondence education has also been widely used in recent years. The Mechanical Engineer Refresher University run by the Ministry of Machine Building enrolls students from all parts of the country through correspondence education. The Shanghai Rubber Industry Company has selected science cadres to participate in correspondence education on rubber technology provided by instructors from the United States. Exploration and innovations in continuing education by central and local TV stations are reflected in lecture series on popularizing microcomputers for specialists and technicians. The Shanghai TV station is now delivering lectures on basic English for scientific specialists, with an audience of 50,000 people. The central TV station has put aside a certain amount of time for continuing education each week.

Study Outside the Working Units. Scientific specialists are sent to higher educational institutions for refresher studies. This is a widely adopted approach in continuing education. For instance, in 1983 and 1984, the Tianjin Design Institute signed a year's contract with Tongji University and five other universities to train eighty-seven mechanical engineers.

Many units send their scientific and advanced specialists abroad to study and do research. For instance, since 1979 the Daqing Oil Administration Bureau has sent 1,000 people abroad to study and do cooperative work in technology. The foreign countries included the United States,

Japan, France, Britain, and West Germany. The Shanghai Heavy Machinery Plant has sent three scientists to pursue study abroad. The China Academy of Sciences and its affiliated organizations have sent 4,000 outstanding scientists abroad as visiting scholars to study for one to two years.

Summary

Postuniversity continuing education or professional continuing education sponsored by the governmental departments, industrial enterprises, research organizations, higher educational institutions, and nongovernmental organizations is developing quickly and drawing more and more attention. The rapid advancement of socioeconomic conditions, science, and technology gives a major impetus to the development of professional continuing education. It is now impossible for professionals or college and university graduates to catch up with the renewal of knowledge without the provision of postuniversity educational programs. So far this work in China is one of the fastest growing segments of adult education.

Zhou Qinggong is a member of the Board of Continuing Engineering Education.

He Jie is head of the Administrative Office of the Nantong City Refresher Institute for Specialists.

The national TV station is now able to show 1,200 hours of educational programs a year. Presently, broadcast and TV universities enroll over 1 million participants; in the last four years 610,000 students have received their university diplomas.

Distance Education

Gao Keming

Overview

China is a developing country with vast land, an enormous population, and an underdeveloped economy and education system. In order to develop the economy and education rapidly, the Chinese government has taken a series of measures. One measure is to fully develop distance education.

Distance education is an important way of enhancing cultural accomplishments and training personnel and has become an important component in the Chinese education system.

China has more than 200 million families. The majority of them have radios, and 30 percent of them have television sets. These possessions have provided a climate for the development of broadcast and TV education.

The major forms of distance education in China include broadcast, TV, correspondence, and newspapers. The educational levels include the regular certified middle and higher education, on-job vocational training, a variety of single-course provisions, and continuing education. According to need and individual conditions, each adult may select the most appropriate educational form and curriculum.

Secondary distance education in China started in the mid 1950s and mainly took the form of correspondence education for training primary school teachers and middle-level technicians. The TV secondary specialized schools began in 1979. Until 1985 there had been 95 TV secondary specialized schools, with a total of 230,000 students. Since 1986 the Central Broadcast and TV University has added the Department of Secondary Specialized Education, which began offering courses in September 1986. The academic majors provided by the department include machinery, electricity, urban architecture, finance and economy, law, and secretarial and teacher education.

In order to meet the needs of economic development in the countryside, the Department of Agriculture, Husbandry, and Fishery, the Department of Education, the Department of Broadcast and TV, and other central government ministries jointly established the Central Agricultural Broadcast School in 1981. It was followed by the establishment of branch schools in more than 2,300 counties (and state farms), 28 provinces, autonomous regions, and municipalities directly under the central government. More than 24,000 villages and rural towns have organized classes in conjuction with the Central Agricultural Broadcast School. Four academic majors—agronomy, agricultural economy, livestock husbandry, and fresh-water fish farming—have been provided for 830,000 participants. By the end of 1985, 75,000 participants received diplomas in secondary specialized school. These graduates have provided 10 percent of the new force in the ranks of agricultural science and technology in China. With the central government, the Central Agricultural Broadcast School has formed a managerial, teaching, and tutorial system for provinces, prefectures, counties, villages, and rural towns. The school is the newest of its type of secondary agricultural school and has the highest enrollments, covering the largest territory in China.

In order to meet the learning needs of various age groups, educational levels, and occupations in the society and to provide educational opportunities for the society, distance education systems have developed rapidly in recent years. Each year the national and local radio and TV stations broadcast a great number and variety of educational programs to meet the varying needs and interests of the people. Between 1978 and 1985, the National TV Station broadcasted 110 educational program sets, with more than 4,000 programs that totaled in excess of 4,000 hours. In 1986 the National TV Station began operating a third channel (to the Beijing area), which has increased the time of TV educational programs from 2.5 to 3.5 hours a day. The National TV Station is now able to show 1,200 hours of educational programs a year. Presently, TV educational programs have developed programs for different audiences, including culture, science, economic management, agriculture and foreign languages. The audience consists of children, young students, adults, senior citizens, teachers, workers, farmers, scientists, and technologists. Available data acquired through the organized viewing of programs show that the most popular programs have more than 1 million viewers, and the least popular programs have more than 100,000 viewers.

Broadcast and TV Universities

Broadcast and TV universities are in the leading position in distance education. At the end of the 1950s and the beginning of the 1960s, the municipalities of Beijing, Tianjin, and Shanghai established broadcast and TV universities, but all closed during the Cultural Revolution. In 1978 the central government approved a proposal for the establishment of broadcast and TV universities. For one year, broadcast and TV universities were established in 28 provinces, autonomous regions (except Tibet), and the municipalities directly under the central government. Courses were formally started in February 1979. In the past eight years, the national network of broadcast and TV universities has conducted six years of formal recruiting, enrolling approximately 1.5 million participants. From this group, 1.2 million have studied in comprehensive programs and 400,000 have studied a single course. There are about 800,000 viewers not formally enrolled but doing self-directed learning. At present, broadcast and TV universities have more than 1 million participants, with an enrollment of 800,000, 350,000 of these being self-directed learners. About 610,000 people enrolled in the previous four years have graduated with university diplomas, and 700,000 have been issued single-course completion certificates. According to the follow-up studies of graduates conducted by local broadcast and TV universities, most participants have reached the required level of training, and their employment units are satisfied.

Broadcast and TV universities, operating for only a few years, have shown such rapid development, enormous enrollment, and great success that they are the subject of attention from educators at home and abroad. Broadcast and TV universities in China are a new type of higher education institution, providing many academic disciplines and majors through distance education by using modern technologies. In the past eight years, broadcast and TV universities have developed six disciplines: science and engineering, education, Chinese, finance and economy, management, and politics and law. There are nineteen academic majors: machine engineering, electrical engineering, chemical engineering, civic architectural engineering, management engineering, math, physics, chemistry (for secondary school science teachers), business management, accounting and auditing, finance, statistics, finance and accounting, Chinese language and literature, journalism, library science, archives, law, and the foundations of management leadership.

Broadcast and TV universities in China operate an administrative system that is well planned and has multilevel course offerings. The criteria for academic planning and graduate requirements are decided and controlled by the Central Broadcast and TV University. Until now, national and local broadcast and TV universities have offered more than 400 courses; 150 foundation and specialized courses were sponsored by the Central Broadcast and TV University. The Central TV Station broadcasts 33 hours of educational programs a week, which are transmitted to the entire nation through a microwave circuit. Since October 1, 1986, the China Education TV Station has been fully operational. The annual hours of educational programs provided by broadcast and TV universities have increased from 1,320 to 3,868. In the meantime, 9 provincial (and municipal) education TV stations, 29 educational program development centers, and 85 learning centers are under construction, being supported by World Bank loans that amount to 37 million U.S. dollars.

Broadcast and TV universities in China have built a high-quality, high-capacity comprehensive program development and transmission system. A network of broadcast and TV education has been formed throughout the nation, with 24,000 faculty and staff, among whom are 11,200 full-time faculty members and 30,000 part-time instructors. More than half of the counties in the nation have set up organizations for broadcast and TV education, supervising more than 30,000 classes in local areas.

The Central Broadcast and TV Normal Institute has been established with the approval of the State Commission on Education. This institute is mainly responsible for the training of secondary and primary school teachers and is now in the process of construction and development.

The Shanghai TV University

The Shanghai TV University (STVU) was established in 1960 and was one of the first institutions of higher education to use modern educational technology. It was forced to close at the beginning of the Cultural Revolution. It reopened in March 1978 and became an independent institution in 1983.

The number of faculty and staff at STVU has increased greatly. At the beginning of its restoration in 1978, there were only 6 full-time faculty and staff members. At present, there are more than 300 full-time faculty and staff members, more than 80 of whom are full-time instructors. More than 40 are distance education researchers and technicians, 100 are administrative personnel, and the rest are staff and workers (including those in the printing plant). A contingent of full-time faculty and staff members is beginning to be established. There are more than 1,100 full-time faculty and staff members at the branches (tutorial stations) in Shanghai.

STVU has developed 8 academic disciplines, with 22 academic majors offering more than 200 courses. More than 24,000 participants from Shanghai have graduated with college diplomas, making up more than one-third of the graduates from the Shanghai adult higher education institutions in the same period. In 1986 more than 9,000 participants in the academic disciplines of finance and economy graduated with college diplomas in the eight academic majors of industrial enterprise management, business enterprise management, industrial accounting, business accounting, statistics, finance and accounting, finance, and material handling. This number is six times the total number of graduates in the academic areas of finance and economy from all higher education institutions in Shanghai in the same year.

Currently, STVU has 16,000 participants formally enrolled and 37,000 self-directed learners. There are 150 branches (tutorial stations) and 700 teaching classes under the Shanghai TV University. Ten suburban counties of Shanghai have set up a branch of the Shanghai TV University, with a collective building space of 17,000 square meters. The branches are the only university outreach for farmers in the rural counties of Shanghai. More than 4,600 participants from these counties have graduated with college diplomas.

Applicants to STVU must meet some requirements. For example, the 1986 general regulations for enrollment at the Shanghai TV University describe the target population and the qualifications needed as follows: "Workers who live in the urban and suburban areas of Shanghai, who have had over two years of employment (started employment before August 31, 1984), and who apply to study the academic majors which are relevant to their industrial enterprises (including collective ownership enterprises, the enterprises run by communes and production brigades in the countryside, and privately owned businesses which have registered at the department of industrial and business administration and management), technicians, cadres, and officers and soldiers of the People's Liberation Army are eligible."

The qualifications for applying for the entrance examinations are "Uphold the Chinese Communist Party; love the motherland, people, and socialism; observe discipline and law; study hard; have high school graduation level or equivalent schooling; have good health enabling one to both work and study; be below the age of forty (born after August 31, 1946). People with infectious diseases, pregnant women, and disabled persons who are not able to take care of their own daily life are not qualified to apply."

STVU mainly uses the following delivery approaches: broadcast (or audiotapes), TV (or videotapes), and a combination of correspondence and face-to-face tutoring. The major links in the teaching process include lectures, self-directed learning, tutoring, discussions, homework, and graduation projects.

Face-to-face instruction and tutorials are extremely important because of the low technical quality of teaching programs on broadcast (audiotapes) and TV (videotapes), which reduces the effectiveness of teaching. Therefore, face-to-face instruction and tutoring make up a relatively high proportion of teaching hours throughout the academic plan.

Most of the tutors are lecturers from regular universities and work on a part-time basis. In order to provide effective tutoring and face-to-face instruction, tutors are trained regularly in the teaching and learning patterns of TV universities. The training provides tutors with information on adult education, familiarizes them with teaching, gives them the opportunity to sample teaching materials and methods, and thus ensures high-quality instruction as well as good teaching and learning techniques. Guidance is also provided through the *Journal of the Shanghai TV University*, which issues a teaching calendar two weeks prior to training. The teaching calendar informs the students and tutors about major broadcasts and TV tutorial content; provides objectives and methods to guide self-directed learners; and also provides clear instructions, content, and objectives for tutors.

The experiments and final fieldwork for students in science and engineering majors are very important links to the teaching and learning process. A cooperative relationship has been established between STVU and regular universities so that experiments required by the curriculum can be carried out in regular universities. Three months of graduate fieldwork usually takes place at the student's working unit or enterprise. Study by students majoring in science and engineering is basically related to their work, and fieldwork is generally arranged at students' working unit. Practice has shown that the graduate field work linkage at STVU has helped students apply the knowledge acquired. Through graduate fieldwork, students in specialized majors have made achievements, and some have even produced outstanding results, which the society appreciates.

STVU has developed multiple levels and models of curriculum materials for college study leading to bachelor of arts or of science degrees, qualification certificates for specialized jobs, and postuniversity continuing education. School operations are more flexible. For example, STVU has established branches in suburban counties and combined self-study through distance learning with self-study examinations administered by the National Advisory Committee on Self-Study Examinations, in cooperation with the Shanghai economic departments training courses offered for specialists. STVU is responsible for producing and broadcasting educational TV programs, and employment units are responsible for organizing courses dealing with requirements for specialized jobs. Students are issued single-course completion certificates after passing the examinations. When the accumulation of academic credits from single-course completion has fulfilled the requirements of their specialized jobs, students are then granted the appropriate qualification certificates.

For eight years, STVU has cooperatively trained more than 24,000 participants. The Shanghai Municipal Bureau of Personnel conducted an evaluation of STVU graduates. A random sample of 9,481 (population of 16,572) was selected. The study indicated that 71 percent of these students had progressed beyond the middle-level job classification, 54 percent beyond the middle-level scientific research capacities, 75 percent beyond the middle-level organizing and managing capacities, 89 percent beyond the middle-level self-directed learning capacities, and 90 percent beyond the middle-level expressing capacities. The results of this analysis show that STVU offers a high quality of education. If written, audio, and video teaching materials can be further adapted to the characteristics of distance education and if a mixture of educational media can be better organized, the education quality at the Shanghai TV University will be further enhanced and comparable to that of regular comprehensive universities.

Summary

The history of higher education through broadcast and TV is short. Due to the urgent need for a large number of personnel for economic construction in China, enrollment was initiated during the process of preparation and development in the field. Teaching materials were borrowed from regular universities. Initially, audio and video teaching materials were not well designed or developed owing to time constraints, and many unsophisticated educational programs were produced. To address these problems, the Central Broadcast and TV University organized curriculum development groups for academic majors and disciplines according to the principles of unified planning. By relying on the strengths of provincial, municipal, and autonomous regional broadcast and TV universities, the broadcast and TV branch of education has grown and developed.

Gao Keming is director of the Research Division of Distance Education at the Shanghai TV University.

The national self-study examinations cover 60 specialized majors. There are 345 examination centers. Currently, there are 3 million examination applicants.

Self-Study Adult Education

Cheng Bingyuan

Development of the Adult Self-Study Examination System

The adult self-study examination system was created in 1981 with the approval of the State Council of the People's Republic of China. In order to encourage the learning and progressive spirit of working personnel and school leaders, to equip personnel with special knowledge, and to develop talented people in the modern construction of China's socialism, the Fifth Plenary Session of the Fifth National People's Congress passed, in 1982, and amendment to the nineteenth item of the Constitution of the People's Republic of China. The amendment reads: "To encourage being a talented person through self-study." Under the supervision and guidance of the Chinese government, the system of self-study examinations is a form of education that combines self-study, "social assisted learning," and state examinations. Among the various forms of education in China, this is the latest educational innovation and has the shortest history.

Social assisted learning means that various social forces provide tutorial activities for self-study through TV, correspondence, face-to-face

Note: The national data in this chapter is from "Self-Study Examinations for Higher Education Have Manifested Great Vitality," *People's Daily,* October 8, 1986, p. 3.

instruction, audiotapes, and videotapes. This instruction is based on requirements in specialized majors, courses, and outlines of self-study examinations. Social assisted learning is an important link between individual self-study and state examinations.

The objectives of the system are to promote broad self-study and social assisted learning activities; train and select capable, specialized personnel; and develop on-job specialized training in postuniversity continuing education through a system of state examinations.

Self-study examinations are divided into examinations for higher education and secondary specialized education. Self-study examinations for higher education are further divided into college level (basic courses) and university diplomas. The content required is similar to that of the traditional curriculum in higher education. The self-study system for higher education is a part of higher education in China; the self-study examinations for secondary specialized education is a part of secondary education, with requirements similar to the regular secondary education.

After two years of pilot testing and three years of experiments, national self-study examinations were well established in 1985. Self-study examinations for higher education have been administered for courses in sixty specialized majors such as arts and science, engineering, agriculture, medicine, finance and economics, politics and law, education and physical education. Currently there are 345 examination locations and 3 million examination applicants. Single-course completion certificates for at least one course have been given to 1.5 million, 150,000 have received single-course completion certificates, and 44,600 have been granted college or university graduation diplomas. Self-study examinations for secondary specialized education started in 1983. By the end of 1985, 17 provinces and municipalities had administered examinations for 27 specialized majors.

Organizations for Self-Study Examinations

The state has developed a network at various organizational levels for self-study examinations. The state has also formulated responsibilities for each organization. The organization of self-study examinations for higher education is the main function of the network. Independent offices have been set up to manage the daily affairs of the self-study examination system for secondary specialized education. Figure 1 shows the organizational structure of the self-study examination system.

The National Advisory Committee on Self-Study Examinations (NACSSE). NACSSE is a state examination organization composed of leaders from related ministries, organizations, and military systems, along with presidents, experts, and professors from institutions of higher education. NACSSE is under the direct leadership of the State Commission

Figure 1. Organizational Structure of the Self-Study Examination System

National advisory committee of self-study examinations
↓
Provincial advisory committees of self-study examinations (for provinces, autonomous regions, and municipalities directly under the central government)
↓ ↓
Prefecture and municipality advisory committees of self-study examinations   Education institutions administering self-study examinations

on Education and reports to the State Planning Commission and Department of Labor and Personnel.

The responsibilities of NACSSE are to

1. Formulate specific directions, policies, and regulations for self-study examinations for higher education according to state educational directives and related policies

2. Guide and coordinate the work of self-study examinations in provinces, autonomous regions, and municipalities directly under the central government

3. Formulate planning principles for administering the examinations of specialized disciplines and to evaluate the provinces, autonomous regions, and municipalities directly under the central government that administer examinations in specialized disciplines

4. Formulate unified criteria for examinations and formulate and evaluate plans for examinations of specialized disciplines in congruence with course outlines and other documents

5. Organize concurrent research in self-study examinations for higher education.

According to the needs of specialized disciplines, the NACSSE has set up a number of committees. The committees are the academic components of the NACSSE and are responsible for developing the examination plans, writing course outlines for self-study examinations, compiling and recommending appropriate learning materials, developing guide books for self-study examinations, and guiding and evaluating the academic work of the examinations within their specialized disciplines as entrusted to them by the NACSSE. So far, 12 working committees of specialized disciplines made up of more than 200 professors and experts have been set up; these cover the disciplines of economic management, Chinese language and literature, philosophy, law, English, civil engineering, mechanical engineering, physics, electronics, agriculture, math, and journalism.

The State Commission on Education has also set up five standing organizations for self-study examinations for higher education for the NACSSE.

Provincial Advisory Committee of Self-Study Examinations (PACSSE). The PACSSE is a provincial-level organization of self-study examinations for higher education and is under both the leadership of the people's government of the provinces, autonomous regions, municipalities, and central government as well as the NACSSE. In China, the PACSSE has been set up in twenty-nine provinces, autonomous regions, and municipalities directly under the leadership of the central government (with the exception of Taiwan province).

The responsibilities of the PACSSE are to

1. Implement the directions and policies of self-study examinations for high education

2. Identify the academic majors for the examinations and to select the educational institutions that administer the examinations under the guidance of the planning principles set by the NACSSE in accordance with local conditions

3. Organize the examinations for specialized majors in local regions

4. Manage examinees' files of examination records and issue single-course completion certificates and graduation diplomas

5. Be entrusted by the NACSSE to guide and supervise the teaching and learning qualities of adult higher education institutions through the method of examinations.

Prefecture and Municipality Advisory Committees of Self-Study Examinations (PMACSSE). The responsibilities of these committees are to organize specific examinations under the leadership of both the local people's governments and the PACSSE, provide management and guidance for social assisted learning in local areas, and organize evaluations of the ideology and morality of the graduates in the local area.

Education Institutions Administering Self-Study Examinations (EIASSE). The EIASSE are selected by the PACSSE from regular institutions of higher education and secondary specialized education that are strong in certain academic disciplines. The EIASSE, under the leadership of the PACSSE, participates in the design and evaluation of examination papers, organizes examinations that require fieldwork, and signs the graduation certificates. By the end of 1985, more than 140 universities and colleges in China had been selected as education institutions to administer self-study examinations.

Methods of Self-Study Examinations

The following are among the methods and requirements of self-study examinations:

1. Any citizen of the People's Republic of China is eligible to apply for the examinations without limits regarding formal schooling and age.

2. Inservice personnel are encouraged to select examinations of specialized majors according to the "principles of studying for the purpose of application."

3. Applicants submit their applications to units identified by the PACSSE or PMACSSE, and qualified applicants are given an examination permit.

4. Graduates with college diplomas from various universities and colleges can apply for self-study examinations in higher education to receive university graduation diplomas.

5. Graduates with university diplomas can apply for self-study examinations for higher education to receive bachelor of arts or of science degrees.

6. Examination halls are generally selected in the cities where the prefecture and municipal governments are located. With the permission of the PACSSE, examination halls can also be selected in counties that are under the leadership of the PMACSSE.

7. Under the guidelines established for standardized examinations, examinations are designed in the following three ways: First, examination papers for the common and required courses and some specialized courses are designed by the NACSSE. Second, examination papers for some basic courses of specialized majors are designed through regional coordination under the unified planning of the NACSSE. Third, examination papers for some basic courses of specialized majors and specialized courses are designed by the PACSSE.

8. The completion period for examinations varies according to specialized majors: college graduation diplomas require two to three years (including basic courses), and university graduation diplomas require three to four years.

9. Those who pass courses are given single-course completion certificates, which are counted as academic credits. Those who accumulate academic credits up to the graduation requirements and pass evaluation on ideology and morality are issued graduation diplomas.

10. People who work in departments directly under specific ministries in the State Council and military systems take examinations at the local site.

Management of the Examination Records

Management of examination records by PACSSE and PMACSSE is an important part of self-study examinations for higher education. After examinees have received one single-course completion certificate, an examinee file is established. A request for changing locations and academic majors should follow the rules in the management of examination records. Any awards or disciplinary actions received during the examination period should be recorded in students' files. Single-course completion certificates of self-study examinations for higher education are recognized throughout China.

After examinees have completed and passed all examinations for required courses in an academic major, examinees' files are comprehensively reviewed and evaluated. Examinees who pass the evaluation are issued graduation diplomas from the appropriate college or university, and their records of schooling are recognized by the state. If examinees meet the requirements of the Academic Degree Regulations of the People's Republic of China according to the examination plans of their academic majors, the accredited institutions that administer examinations have the authority to confer B.A. or B.S. degrees on examinees.

Guidelines for Self-Study Examinations

Advisory committees for self-study at all levels have set up strict disciplinary guidelines and measures to evaluate implementation. People considered violators of the disciplines are (1) those who do not follow the regulations and evaluation procedures set by the NACSSE; (2) those who do not have approval to start the examinations for a new academic major or lower the criteria for the examinations; (3) those who receive graduation diplomas but who actually fail to meet the requirements for the evaluations; (4) those who discuss the examination questions and violate the discipline in the examination halls.

Self-Study Examinations in Shanghai

In accordance with the requirements of the Tentative Methods of the Self-Study Examinations for Higher Education approved by the State Council, self-study examinations for higher education in Shanghai began in 1982 and have been administered twice a year. The following eleven institutions of higher education have been selected by the Shanghai Advisory Committee on Self-Study Examinations for Higher Education to administer the examinations: East China Normal University, the Shanghai Institute of Education, the Shanghai Institute of Foreign Languages, the Shanghai Institute of Economics and Finances, Fudan University, the Shanghai Transportation University, East China Institute of Politics and Law, the College of Arts at Shanghai University, the College of Electronic Machinery at Shanghai Engineering and Technology University, the Shanghai Industrial University, and the Shanghai Institute of Foreign Trade. By June 1986 examinations for 21 academic majors had been administered, with 262,000 examinees, of whom more than 211,200 had received single-course completion certificates.

Examinations of all academic majors are administered in accordance with the examination plans and course outlines for self-study examinations. Ten to fourteen examination courses are required for junior college graduate diplomas, and credits are based on the accumulation of single-course completions. After examinees have passed the graduation evaluation and if ideology and morality evaluation requirements are fulfilled, examinees are issued junior college graduation diplomas in self-study examinations for higher education. About twenty examination courses are required for university graduation diplomas. According to the requirements of the examination plans for the university graduation diplomas, examinees who have received junior college graduation diplomas may take six more required examination courses and three elective examination courses. If they pass the graduation evaluation and the ideology and morality evaluation, examinees will be issued university graduation diplomas for higher education. For example, according to the plan of self-study examinations in the academic major of Chinese language and literature at the Shanghai Institute of Education, examinees for junior college graduation diplomas must pass ten examination courses in philosophy, history of the Chinese Communist Party (or political economy), modern Chinese language, ancient Chinese language, introduction to literature, selected works in modern Chinese literature, selected works of ancient Chinese literature, foreign literature, writing, and theory of education. A total of 74 academic credits are accumulated based on these courses. A total of 130 academic credits are accumulated based on single-course completion. According to the plan of self-study examinations in the English major, examinees must pass three commomly required courses in philosophy, history of the Chinese Communist Party, university-level Chinese language, and the eight required courses for the English major. A total of 70 academic credits are accumulated on the basis of single-course completion.

By June 1986 more than 2,800 people in Shanghai were issued junior college graduation diplomas on completion of the overall evaluation of their examination files.

Self-study examinations for secondary specialized education are also an important part of the system of self-study examinations and of secondary specialized education in China. With the approval of the Shanghai People's Government, self-study examinations for secondary specialized education in Shanghai started in 1984. As of June 1986, examinations for sixteen academic majors in five academic disciplines of finance and economics, politics and law, medicine, architectural engineering, and education were administered by selected educational institutions. The examination completion period is generally three years, and examinations are administered twice a year. The number of examination courses varies from twelve to thirteen, according to the academic major plan. The common cultural courses and basic courses for specialized majors are required, and make up 70 percent of the total number of courses. Specialized courses make up 30 percent, and there is one elective course. For example, the examination plan for the industrial accountant major in the discipline of economic management requires that examinees take eight commonly required examination courses, which include philosophy, political economy, Chinese, math, accounting, statistics, computer technology, economics, and three specialized required courses in industrial accounting, industrial finance, and analysis of the economic activities of industrial enterprises. Examinees are also required to elect one course in management of accounts, finance and loans, and financial math. Examinees are issued single-course completion certificates if they pass the examinations. Those who fail do not have a second chance to take the examinations. After examinees have passed all the examinations according to the examination plan and the overall evaluation of their ideology and morality, they are issued graduation diplomas of self-study examinations for secondary specialized education. By the end of June 1986, examinees numbered 170,000, and it is anticipated that 10,000 people will receive graduation diplomas in the next year.

Cheng Bingyuan is deputy director of the Office of the Shanghai Admission Committee for Higher Education.

Part 3.

Professional Preparation and Research

To meet the needs of the field, ten normal schools in adult higher education have been established throughout China for the special purpose of training teachers and administrators of adult education.

Professional Preparation of Adult Educators

Jiang Keyi, Lin Weihua

Background

The Chinese government has expressed its commitment to (1) establish a professional group of full-time and part-time adult educators; (2) employ full-time teachers at the proportion of 3 to 5 percent of the total number of workers; (3) dispatch university graduates to adult schools as teachers; (4) provide university and college refresher courses for teachers in adult schools; (5) treat adult teachers as equals to technicians and engineers in promotion, salary raises, bonuses, and welfare rewards; and (6) confer professional titles according to the same standards as the formal school system. These regulations have helped build a contingency of teachers and administrators for adult education. However, the development and expansion of adult education in China has happened so rapidly, that many of these regulations have not been completely followed.

For several years adult educators and administrators have come mainly from the following sources (1) technicians and engineers of industrial or business enterprises; (2) people from other administrative areas; (3) teachers of various formal school systems; and (4) teachers and administrators who have long engaged in vocational education. Although these professional groups have played an important role in the development of adult education in China, there are serious limitations. Chiefly, most practitioners lack experience in adult education; do not have much professional background; lack understanding of the nature, status, function, and characteristics of adult education; and have never studied theory, psychology, or administrative theory of adult education.

To meet the needs of the developing field, normal schools in adult higher education have been established in some areas in China for the purpose of training adult teachers and administrators. These institutions include the Shanghai Second Institute of Education, the Hefei Institute of Education in eastern China, the Chengdu Institute of Adult Education, the Yongchuang Branch School of Chongqing Institute of Education in western China, the Guangzhou Institute of Education in southern China, the Wuhan Institute of Adult Education in middle China, the Beijing Institute of Adult Education in northern China, and the Harbin City Institute of Adult Education and the Changchuen City Broadcasting and Correspondence Institute in northeast China. These institutions are gradually becoming the training bases for teachers and administrators in adult education.

The National Cooperative Association

There is frequent communication among these institutes, and mutually cooperative relationships have developed. In 1984 the Shanghai Second Institute of Education and the Chengdu Institute of Adult Education set up the National Cooperative Association. In October 1984 the first annual conference of the National Cooperative Association was held in Shanghai. The second annual conference was held in Chengdu in December 1985. At these two conferences, participants discussed such important issues as educational methodologies and instructional experiences of the institutes of adult education. Participants also investigated the possibilities and strategies of further cooperation among institutes. During the period between the two conferences, the institutes organized several special meetings on specific subject areas. At these meetings, programs of various subject areas were carefully discussed and revised, and some textbooks were cooperatively pre-edited to meet special concerns of adult learning.

The preparatory meeting for the third annual conference of the National Cooperative Association was held from January 6 to 9, 1987, in Wuhan. In attendance were either the presidents or vice-presidents of the various institutes. At the planning meetings, participants discussed the documents of the Yantai Conference (the National Working Conference of Adult Education held previously at Yantai), reviewed work that had been done since the second annual conference, developed the agenda for the third annual conference, and divided responsibilities among individual members. The planners selected the theme and goal for the third annual conference: "study and implement the document of the Yantai Conference and work toward raising the quality of the adult education programs in the institutes." The main topics proposed for future discussion and study at the conference were "how to reform and develop the institutes of adult education under the new modernization policies" and "to investigate and design a professional training program for full-time administrators and full-time and part-time teachers in adult education." The cooperative tasks of the institutes will be to "exchange domestic and international information on adult education," "improve the practice of adult educational administration," "further revise the programs of the six subjects offered by the institutes of adult education," and "organize the procedures of editing textbooks." The topics and reports presented at the third annual conference were

1. Main Topics
    - Review of the work done since the second annual conference
    - Report on and discussion of the Yantai Conference document
    - Reformation and development of the institutes of adult education (main topic)
    - Tentative consideration of the professional training programs for full-time administrators, full-time teachers, and part-time teachers in the institutes of adult education (main topic)
    - Reports on the progress of cooperative programs developed by the second annual conference, discussion of the scheme for further cooperation, and some items for the fourth annual conference.
2. Information Exchanged
    - Report on criteria for promotion and employment of professors and staff
    - Report on the experiment of promoting the credit system in the institutes of adult education
    - Report on the establishment of the subject area of adult education administration
    - Developmental trends in international adult education
    - Report on the professional training program for high-level adult educators and administrators
    - Shifting focus of faculty in adult education to serve professional training programs.

The Shanghai Second Institute of Education

Shanghai is the largest industrial city in China. Comparatively, the economy, culture, education, science, and technology in Shanghai are well developed. Adult education in Shanghai has developed rapidly because of a large work force and the subsequent need for training adult teachers and administrators. In 1981 the Shanghai Municipal Government decided to establish a teacher training (normal) school specializing in adult education: the Shanghai Second Institute of Education. The municipal government listed the Second Institute's tasks: "to train teachers for workers' and peasants' nonformal education; to train teachers for middle-level on-job professional education; to develop a new way of training based on the unique characteristics of adults; to become a research center for workers' nonformal education and professional adult education in the Shanghai area; to become a center for books and materials on adult education and instructional research; and to promote the development of workers' nonformal education and professional education." In 1983 the municipal government further determined that the Second Institute should be "a training center for the teachers of workers' and peasants' secondary education for the whole city." In 1984 the Conference of Worker Education in Shanghai stressed that the Second Institute "should be urged to initiate the four-year collegiate program, and to actively undertake the tasks of training the administrators in adult education." In recent years, the Second Institute has not only offered educational services for the Shanghai area but for the Shanghai Economic Zone as well as some remote areas. The Second Institute is showing high potential and is gradually becoming a normal school of adult education, with departments in liberal arts, natural sciences, engineering, and administration. It has been accredited by the State Commission of Education.

Vital Statistics. The Shanghai Second Institute of Education is located in northeast Shanghai. The campus area covers 2,800 square meters. The new physics-chemistry building and electrical engineering building have just been constructed and put into use. There are 29 labs equipped with advanced instruments. The library building occupies a total space of 4,300 square meters and has 320,000 books and 2,000 periodicals in native and foreign languages. In addition to the reading rooms for faculty and students, the library also has photocopy machines for client use, as well as audiovisual teaching facilities equipped with VCR, camera, slide equipment, and audiovisual production equipment. The printing workshop has more than forty workers, who undertake the tasks of printing textbooks, teaching materials, and the journal of the institute, as well as contracting services to other units. But the present resources of the Second Institute are far from satisfying the needs encountered by the rapid development of adult education. According to the five-year plan of the institute, the area of the Second Institute is to be enlarged by as much as 63,000 square meters, and the number of facilities doubled by the year 1990.

Staff and Curriculum. Through the great efforts of faculty and staff, ten departments have been established, including political education, chinese literature, foreign languages, adult educational administration, mathematics, physics, chemistry, physical education, mechanics, and electrical engineering. A Department of Civil Engineering is under development. These departments all train adult teachers within their areas. The training goals are to make participants capable of engaging not only in instruction but also in administrative or technological work. Additionally, the Shanghai Adult Education Research Institute is situated in the Second Institute. The Research Institute is under the dual leadership of the Shanghai Bureau of Education and the Second Institute. In the Research Institute there are sixteen researchers and specialists in adult education. Their research covers fundamental theories of adult education, policy trends in Chinese adult education, history of Chinese adult education, and adult education laws and regulations. The Research Institute is actively developing cooperative relationships with domestic and international research institutions.

There are about 540 faculty and staff now at the institute, including 280 full-time teachers and more than 30 professors and associate professors. About 40 members of the faculty are currently studying for doctoral or master's degrees or preparing for a lecturer certificate in domestic or international universities. The institute invites an educational expert from the United States and 15 professors from other universities to be area advisers for its different departments.

Students. There are more than 2,000 four-year and three-year students undertaking full-time study, semi-off-job study, and nonformal study. Instruction is mainly in the classroom. Students come from various adult schools, a variety of levels, and, for the most part, are on-job teachers or administrators. Two to three hundred students recommended by their work units come from the remote provinces or regions of the country. After taking the National Entrance Examination of the Colleges and Universities of Adult Education conducted once every year, these students are admitted for their high performance on the examination. Tuition and fees are paid by their work units. After several years of systematic training, students return to their jobs in their former work units.

During the past years, 3,000 three-year students graduated from the different departments of the institute. Surveys show that most of the graduates on return are judged to be capable, enjoy their work, and perform well at their jobs. Quite a few graduates have become core members of the faculty; some are elected leaders of their schools, and some are selected to enter the leading circles of enterprises, companies, or governmental bureaus.

Programs. In order to better adjust to the economic development of society, the Second Institute has been trying several experimental instructional programs, with good results.

In addition to the degree programs mentioned above, the institute also provides short-term or single-subject programs. In the latter half of 1986, for example, the different departments of the institute not only assumed the responsibility of teaching more than 2,000 students in degree programs but also initiated more than 10 various short-term training courses that attracted more than 3,500 participants.

Beginning in the autumn of 1986, the institute offered various training courses leading to certificates for different job positions. The courses certify (1) professional positions of machine building within Shanghai business and industries; (2) educational administrative positions within the city's textile mills; and (3) English training within the city's oceanic transportation companies.

Participants do not need high grades for admission, but they are required to have the equivalent of college-level professional knowledge. These adult education programs are now experimental, but according to the National Working Conference of Adult Education policies, these programs will be a large part of China's adult education.

Continuing Education. In addition to these different programs, the Second Institute is also working on postuniversity continuing education. As a highly regarded institute of adult education in the country, the Second Institute is responsible for and required to train intellectuals of high professional level and to especially contribute to the training of administrators in the field of adult education. In May 1986 the institute initiated an Adult Education Theory Seminar which is a high-level course. The length of the seminar was three weeks. Forty-seven participants came from fourteen provinces and cities such as Inner Mongolia, Yunnan, Guangdong, Guangxi, Sichuan, and Jilin, and from the departments of adult education in such enterprises as the processing industry, building and construction, and finance enterprises in Shanghai.

International Relations. The Shanghai Second Institute of Education emphasizes cooperation and communication with domestic and international educational institutions, research institutions, and academic organizations in the field of adult education. It also emphasizes learning from experience in the development of adult education and the training needs of teachers and administrators in both domestic and international institutions. In recent years the institute has welcomed several dozen experts, professors, and practitioners of adult education from the United States, Canada, Japan, West Germany, and Australia to discuss topics and issues in the field of adult education. In May 1986 the institute dispatched a delegation to the United States to attend the Adult Education Research Conference of North America. At the conference the Chinese delegates introduced information on adult education in China and contacted many international colleagues. Also, a formal exchange agreement between the Second Institute and Northern Illinois University was signed, providing a good starting point for further cooperation between the two institutions.

Future Directions. To adjust to the new circumstances of economic construction, the institute has begun to plan for future subject needs in ten departments. The initial ideas are to emphasize concrete application of liberal arts and natural sciences; consolidate the construction of the various management courses; encourage cooperation among the departments; design new curricula to better meet the needs of society; and plan new programs urgently needed by society. The new programs will be based on experiences with previously offered short courses and will depend on accumulating information and recruiting able professors and professional members. Not only will the programs have the characteristics of adult normal education but they also will have the function of serving the economy and the society.

Summary

The Second Institute has been a formal institution of adult education for only six years. Although it has achieved some success in training adult teachers and administrators, it still has a long way to go in adapting to the rapid development of the adult education movement in China. Now the faculty and staff of the institute are working diligently to accomplish the five-year plan for the development of the institute and to achieve the goal of turning the institute into a first-rate, well-advanced training base for adult educators and administrators in China.

Jiang Keyi is deputy director of the Department of Adult Education Administration of the Shanghai Second Institute of Education.

Lin Weihua is vice-president of the Shanghai Second Institute of Education.

In order to strengthen adult education research and theoretical study, the people's government organized a number of research organizations, all with full-time researchers.

Research and Adult Education

Sun Shilu

China's adult education, known presently for its large-scale practice, has a long history. However, research lags behind the practice and zigzags forward slowly. Since the 1980s research and theoretical study have accelerated, the scope of study has been extended, more organizations have been formed, and achievements have increased. Though no perfect theoretical system has been formed, study and research have obviously influenced practice.

This chapter focuses on the organizations, topics, findings, and effects on the practice of adult education research in China.

Organizations

To keep pace with economic modernization, adult education in China has been developing rapidly. Problems encountered in practice need to be addressed through theoretical study and research. Theory is also needed in policymaking. The growth in practice has driven research forward, and individuals from all levels have shown an interest in theory. However, most researchers are adult education program administrators and teachers who engage in research and theoretical study in their spare time.

To strengthen research and theoretical study, the government formed a number of research organizations such as the Beijing Adult

Education Research Center, the Tianjin Adult Education Research Center, the Shanghai Adult Education Research Institute, and the Shanghai Workers' Higher Education Research Center. All research organizations have full-time researchers. Parallel to these organizations are academic societies and associations in all parts of China.

Several national organizations have been formed, including the Chinese Adult Education Association, the Chinese Worker Education Research Society, the Chinese Continuing Engineering Education Institute, and the Chinese Vocational Training Institute. Many local organizations have joined the Chinese Adult Education Association and the Chinese Worker Education Research Society, which are the most influential organizations in China.

The Chinese Worker Education Research Society. This society was founded in 1984. The nature, purposes, tasks, membership, organization, and financing of the society are discussed in the sections below.

Nature. The society is an academic organization that adheres to the guiding ideology that education must be geared to the needs of modernization for the world and the future. The society promotes and develops education for workers.

Purposes. The society upholds the principles of seeking truth from facts and integrating theory with practice. It carries out the policy of "letting a hundred flowers blossom and a hundred schools of thought contend" and advocates academic democracy. It promotes the development of education for workers and accelerates socialist modernization.

Tasks. First, through research in education for workers, the society provides the theoretical and practical basis for guiding the practice of education for workers and sets forth the principles, policies, laws, and regulations concerning education for workers. It aims at the gradual establishment of a Chinese theoretical system of education for workers. Second, the society discusses and draws up plans for research in worker education and organizes and promotes research activities. Third, the society gradually is enlarging its organization and building a research contingent of a fairly high-level staff composed of full-time and part-time researchers. Fourth, the society organizes the publication of periodicals and books and introduces and disseminates research findings. Finally, the society arranges exchanges with foreign countries.

Membership. The society is composed mainly of group members. Worker education research organizations and adult education organizations at or above the prefectural (city) level, large key enterprises, universities and colleges, mass organizations or democratic parties, which accept the society's regulations and apply for membership, can be accepted as group members with the approval of the secretariat.

The society also accepts a limited number of individuals as members. Specialists and scholars who devoted themselves to worker education and have made some contribution in research can become individual members through application and approval of the secretariat.

Members have the right to participate in activities organized by the society and to give their opinions and suggestions. They are to report their work, research activities, and findings regularly to the society.

Organization. The society has a number of honorary presidents and advisers. The leading body of the society is the council. Members of the council are selected through consultation from concerned departments. The term of office is three years and may be renewed.

The council exercises the following rights: to decide the society's guidelines, tasks, and working plans; to examine the work reports of the standing council; to elect members of the standing council and officers of the society. The standing council exercises the rights of the council and executes resolutions when the council is not in session.

The secretariat is the administrative body of the council. It has a liaison department, an academic research department, and an editorial and publishing department; these deal with the daily work with guidance from the secretary general and the deputy secretary general.

Financing. Funds are allocated to the society by the government, and donations are made by members.

The organizational structure of the society is seen in Figure 1.

Since its founding, the society has organized many activities and is growing rapidly. At present, it has 180 group members, and its research network extends all over the country, including individual enterprises.

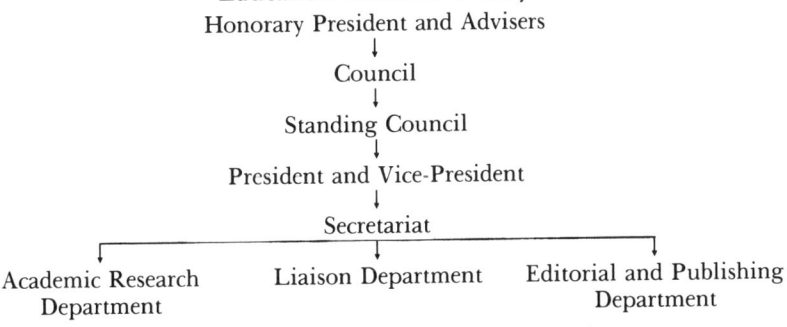

Shanghai Adult Education Research Society. This society was founded in 1983. It is a group member of both the Chinese Adult Education Association and the Chinese Worker Education Research Society. Within the society, three groups have been formed: the Worker Secondary Education Group, the Peasant Education Group, and the Adult Higher Education Group. The society has 280 individual and 12 group members, which include the Worker Education Study Society of Shanghai Third Iron and Steel Plant, Adult Education Research Group of Changning

Figure 1. Organizational Structure of the Chinese Worker Education Research Society

Honorary President and Advisers
↓
Council
↓
Standing Council
↓
President and Vice-President
↓
Secretariat

| Academic Research Department | Liaison Department | Editorial and Publishing Department |

district of Shanghai, the Shanghai Adult Foreign Language Teaching Society, and the Adult Education Research Society of Chuansha county.

More than 1,000 adult educators and practitioners have been organized by the society and they engage in research in their spare time.

Shanghai Adult Education Research Institute. Located on the campus of the Shanghai Second Institute of Education, this institute was founded in 1982. It is under the dual leadership of the Shanghai Education Bureau and the Shanghai Second Institute of Education. The task of this institute is to work on adult education theory and to collect and organize information and data about adult education service. It has sixteen full-time researchers. Presently, its research includes such areas as foundation theory of adult education, administration of adult education, methodology of adult education, adult learning psychology, history of adult education, teaching methods and materials of adult education, comparative adult education, worker education in large- and medium-sized enterprises, and peasant education.

The institute has established many connections both at home and abroad. It is also a group member of the Chinese Worker Education Research Society. The director of the institute is a member of the National Education Science Leading Group under the State Commission on Education, a member of the standing council of the Chinese Worker Education Research Society, and a member of the Council of the National Comparative Education Research Society. The deputy director is the secretary general of the Shanghai Adult Education Research Society. The institute has established connections with over thirty countries or regions and with international adult education research organizations.

Adult Education Research

Topics and Findings. In recent years, the scope of research has grown. At the 1983 conference of the Chinese Adult Education Association, participants exchanged views on research topics. They agreed that research should begin with a summary of experiences since the founding of New China, focus on the solution of the problems encountered in practice, and gradually establish a Chinese adult education theory system with Chinese characteristics. The following are a collection and organization of the topics presented and agreed on by the participants:

- Concept, nature, status, function, purpose, task, characteristics, and principles of adult education
- Adult education and construction of material and spiritual civilization
- Adult education and intelligence development
- Economic benefit of adult education
- Present state and future development of China's adult education
- Chinese adult educational system

- Leading system of China'a adult education
- Policies and principles of China's adult education
- Purpose, content, and period of study of adult education institutions
- Regularization of worker education
- Purpose, content, and form of cadre education and training
- Ways of updating knowledge of scientists and technicians
- Development of adult teachers
- Organizations and research personnel
- Adult education legislation
- Consolidation and development of double remedial worker education
- Relationship of basic, technical, political, and ideological education
- Application and development of audiovisual aids in adult education
- Character, laws, policies, guidelines, tasks, principles, and content of peasant education under the "four modernizations"
- Provision of adult education programs in frontier and minority areas
- Provision of primary and secondary cultural and technical education programs in rural areas
- Form, teaching materials, results, recognition, consolidation, and development of literacy
- Collection and organization of local and national adult education historical data
- Psychology of adult learners
- Teaching guidelines, tasks, process, principles, content, and methods in adult education
- Evaluation of teaching materials in adult schools
- Measurement of adult learning achievement
- Administration of adult schools
- Adult independent study and its guidance.

In 1986 the Chinese Worker Education Research Society suggested that members of the society choose the following topics for more research:

- Principles of worker education
- Relationship among national economy, social development, and worker education
- System of worker education
- Content and teaching methods in worker education
- Political and ideological education for workers
- Administration of worker education
- Development and employment of administrators and teachers in worker education

- Worker education abroad
- Worker education legislation
- History of worker education
- Theory of worker education.

Often, researchers choose their own topics and work on them independently. Sometimes, however, leading bodies such as educational departments, bureaus, or research organizations organize some researchers to work on certain priority topics. For instance, the Chinese Worker Education Research Society gathered sixty researchers together in 1984 and divided them into four groups to do research on the nature, characteristics, status, function, economic benefits, regularization, and structure of worker education. The Shanghai Worker Education Research Institute jointly worked on legislation and drafted the Working Regulations of Shanghai Worker Education. The State Commission on Education organized a nationwide survey on the present state of adult education in 1986.

Research papers presented to annual conferences all over the country have been increasing in recent years. An example is the annual conference of the Chinese Worker Education Research Society, which in 1985 received 1,943 papers. Several books on adult education have also been published in recent years. Some constructs raised by the authors of the papers and books have been commonly agreed on, namely that

1. The development of adult education is controlled and influenced by a variety of factors such as politics, economy, and culture.

2. Adult education is bound to develop, and nothing can prevent this trend.

3. Any education, whether it is child or adult education, shares its common characteristics with other forms of education but also has its own special characteristics.

4. Although education in different countries shares common characteristics, a general model probably does not exist.

5. China's adult education must suit the Chinese context.

6. Adult education must be diversified.

7. Adult education must focus on the needs of society, organizations, and individuals.

Effects of Research on Practice. The findings of research reach practice through various channels. At present, there are at least thirty magazines devoted to adult education. Some are published for the general public, but most are for internal reference. Examples of the former are *Adult Education* (Heilongjiang Province), *Beijing Adult Education, Tainjin Adult Education, Shanghai Education: Worker and Peasant Edition, Shandong Worker Education, Intelligence Development* (Wuhan), and *Higher Adult Education Studies* (East China Normal University). Two other journals, *Education Research* and *Foreign Education*, also publish some articles on adult education.

Workshops using findings from research are continually organized to train adult education administrators and teachers. For instance, a workshop was organized by the Chinese Worker Education Research Society at Dalian in 1985. Over 100 participants, most of whom were administrators from large enterprises all over the country, attended the workshop.

Papers, presentations, and suggestions at the annual conferences all over the country are organized and sent to the government for reference on policy making. The findings gained from research work organized or sponsored by the government have a more direct influence on policy making.

The effects of research on practice cannot be accurately estimated at present. However, some effects are obvious. Research findings help to raise the status of adult education. More and more people are realizing the importance of adult education and invest in it. Research findings begin to penetrate into the realm of policy making, and some have already become policies of the government. For example, a Decision on the Formation and Development of Adult Education has been drafted at the recent National Adult Educators Conference and will be officially adopted and promulgated by the State Council. Research findings help practitioners do their jobs better.

Problems and Trends. Although the research contingent is large, the time involved in research is not long enough, and most researchers do research in their spare time. Most have not had enough training in research and are learning by doing. The number of full-time researchers is too small.

Another problem is that researchers have not done enough work on environmental and controlling factors of adult learning or instructional methodology. Fortunately, some organizations have put these kinds of topics on their research agendas, and it can be predicted that research in these areas will grow.

We still lack a national, systematic organization, editing, and publication of adult education materials. Statistical data are scarce. These limitations are disadvantages to researchers. National adult education organizations must address these problems.

Research methodology must be modernized. Some research organizations wish to install modern equipment but lack funds to do so. Along with the development of the economy and the realization of the importance of adult education, research funds may increase, and methodology and equipment may improve.

Although the above-mentioned problems exist, a foundation has been laid in adult education research and theoretical study.

Sun Shilu is a member of the National Education Science Leading Group under the State Commission of Education and a member of the Standing Council of the Chinese Worker Education Research Society.

Index

A

Academic Degree Regulations of the People's Republic of China, 104
Adult education: achievements of, 6-7; characteristics of, 9; development periods in, 6-7; functions of, 8-9; guidelines of, 9-10; history of, 5-8; job-related competence in, 9; leadership in, 10; learning activities in, 10; and lifelong education, 10-11; magazines devoted to, 122; problems and trends of, 123; provisions for, 9-10; rapid rise in, 7; research topics and findings, 120-123; in Shanghai, 67-73; social context of, 5-11; status of, 8; system diagram, 3
Adult education in universities. *See* University adult education
Adult educators, 109-115; background of, 109-110; sources for, 109-111; state regulations for, 109; training bases for, 110
Anti-Japanese War: and cadre education, 45, 46; and literacy education, 6
Art training, as social education, 56-57
Australia, 114

B

Book reading and review, as social education, 55
Broadcast education. *See* Distance education
Broadcast and TV Universities, 93-94; administrative system of, 93-94; disciplines in, 93; staff at, 94

C

Cadre, definition of, 45
Cadre education, 45-51; in Chuansha, 27-28; content of, 47-48; party schools in, 48-49; purpose of, 47; Shanghai Party School as, 49-51; training institutions for, 48
Cai Y. (Renzi), 5
Canada, 114
Central Agricultural Broadcasting School, 28, 92; Chuansha Branch School of, 30; in Jilin Province, 20
Central Agriculture Department, 30
Central Broadcast and TV Normal Institute, 94
Central Broadcast and TV University, 91-92, 93-94, 97
Central Committee of the Chinese Communist Party (CCCCP), and cadre education, 45, 46-47, 49
Central Department of Cadre Education, 45-46
Central Fishery Department, 30
Central People's Radio Station, 30
Central TV Station, 94
Changning District First Spare-Time Secondary School, as institutional school, 70-71
Changning District Worker Secondary Technical School, as institutional school, 71
Chen G., 49
Chen P., 49
China Academy of Sciences, and continuing education, 85, 87-88, 89
China Education TV Station, 94
Chinese Adult Education Association, 118, 120-121
Chinese Association of the Blind and Deaf, 60
Chinese Communist Party (CCP), and cadre education, 45, 46-47, 48, 49, 50
Chinese Continuing Engineering Education Association, 37-38
Chinese Education Center for the Handicapped, 61
Chinese Education Society, 5
Chinese People's Political Consultative Conference (CPPCC), and cadre education, 45

Chinese Science and Technology Association, 85-86
Chinese Vocational Education Society, 5
Chinese Welfare Foundation for the Handicapped, 60, 61
Chinese Worker Education Research Society, 118-119, 120; constructs of, 122; organizational structure of, 119; and topics, 121-122; workshop, 123
Chou E., and study-work movement, 6
Chuansha: correspondence school in, 27; peasant education in, 25-31; peasant secondary and technical education in, 28-31; remedial education in, 27-28; social culture and life education in, 30-31; and worker technical education, 26-27
Circular of Admission and Graduate Placement of the Handicapped Youth in Higher Education Institutions, 59-60
Civil Affairs Administration, and special education, 60
Compulsory Education Act of the People's Republic of China, and special education, 59
Confucius, 10
Constitution of China, and literacy education, 15
Continuing education, 8, 83-89; and academic associations and democratic parties, 85-86; academic exchange in, 88; agencies for, 83-86; basic approaches of, 87-89; for career change, 86; classroom sessions in, 87; and foreign country exchange, 88-89; and governmental structuring, 83-84; and higher educational institutions, 84-85; and industrial enterprises, 84; lectures in, 87-88; and new technology, 86-87; and research, 87; and research organizations, 84-85; self-study, correspondence, and TV education in, 88; at Shanghai Second Institute of Education, 114; study outside working units in, 88-89; supplementary programs in, 86; types of programs in, 86-87

Correspondence education; admission requirements in, 77; costs of, 79; funding for, 78; instruction methods for, 77-78; program planning in, 77; teachers and stations for, 78; textbooks for, 77; Tongji University, as example of, 78-79; in universities, 76-79. See also Distance education
Cultural activities. See Social education
Cultural Revolution: and cadre education, 46-47; and distance education, 93; and handicapped, 62; and literacy, 16; and peasant education, 29; and university adult education, 75-76; and worker education, 34. See also Ten Year Chaos

D

Decision on Large-Scale Development of Correspondence Education and Evening College in Universities, 76
Decision on Literacy, 15
Decision for On-Job Training for Cadres, 46
Decision on the Reformation of the Education System: and special education, 59; and worker education, 34
Decision on the Strengthening of Worker Education, 34
Decisions on the Regularization of Party Schools Education, 47
Decisions on the Work of Cadre Education Within the Party, 47
Department of Agriculture, Husbandry, and Fishery, 92
Department of Broadcast and TV, 92
Department of Civil Administration, and special education, 61
Department of Civil Affairs, and special education, 59-60
Department of Education, 92
Department of Labor, and special education, 59-60
Department of Secondary Specialized Education, 91-92
Directives for Literacy, 15-16
Directives on Strengthening the Education for Cadres, 46

Distance education, 91-97; overview of, 91-93. *See also* Correspondence education

E

Education Institutions Administering Self-Study Examinations (EIASSE), 102
Exhibitions, as social education, 55

F

Fifth Plenary Session of the Fifth National People's Congress, and self-study examinations, 99
First Auto Plant: degree education for workers at, 36-37; educational awards at, 35, 37; inservice worker degree education at, 35-36; nondegree education at, 37-38; principle of learning at, 35; and worker education, 34-38
First Revolutionary Civil War, and cadre education, 6
Forty-Fourth amendment, and special education, 59
France, 51

G

Germany, 51
Government Organizations of the Central Committee, 47
Guo K., 36

H

Handicapped people: education of, 60-63; and unemployment, 61-63. *See also* Special education
Handicapped Student Association, 60
Hobby activities, as social education, 55-56
Hungary, 51
Husbandry Department, 30

I

Industrial enterprises, and continuing education, 84
Inservice training. *See* Worker education

Institutional education, 67-73; background of 67; diplomas and certificates for, 69; and examinations, 69; and funding, 68-69; and teachers, 68; textbooks for, 69
Instructors. *See* Adult educators International Literacy Award Committee, 17
Italy, 51

J

Japan, 51, 114
Jilin Province: instruction flexibility and practicality in, 18-19; literacy plans and rules in, 17-18; literacy principles in, 18; literacy program in, 17-20; literacy quality control in, 18; and populace mobilization, 19-20; postliteracy education in, 20

K

Ke Q., 49
Korea, 51

L

Lectures, as social education, 55
Lifelong education, 10-11
Literacy education, 8, 15-21; background of, 15-17; and the handicapped, 62; and illiteracy rates, 16; in Jilin Province, 17-20; principles for, 15-16. *See also* Peasant education
Literature writing, as social education, 56
Liu C., 49
Liu X., 49
Lu S., 10
Luwan District Spare-Time University, as institutional school, 73

M

Mao Z., 46
Music, as social education, 56-57

N

National Adult Education Conference, 8

National Advisory Committee on Self-Study Examinations (NACSSE), 100-101, 102, 103, 104; responsibilities of, 101; and STVU, 96
National Cooperative Association: and adult educators, 110-111; and conference topics, 111
National Economy Committee, 7
National People's Congress, and cadre education, 45
National Planning Committee, and special education, 59-60
National Science Committee, 37-38
National TV Station, 92-93
New Democratic Revolution, and adult education, 6
Newspapers as education. *See* Distance education

O

Old Democratic Revolution, 5-6

P

Party schools: and cadre education, 48-49; training content at, 49. *See also* Shanghai Party School
Peasant education, 20-21, 23-31; changes in, 23; in Chuansha County, 25-31; economic development in, 23-25; guidelines for, 21; and labor force shift, 24; science and technology in, 24-25; in Shanghai suburbs, 25; vocational education in, 21; and Zinan County example, 24-25
Peng C., 49
Performing arts, as social education, 56-57
Postliteracy education, 20-21
Postuniversity education, 83-89. *See also* Continuing education
Prefecture and Municipality Advisory Committees of Self-Study Examinations (PMACSSE), 102, 103
Principles of the Program for Nationwide Cadre Training, 47
Provincial Advisory Committee of Self-Study Examinations (PACSSE), 102, 103; responsibilities of, 102

R

Remedial education, in Chuansha, 27-28
Renzi Outline, 5
Research, 117-123; and continuing education, 84-85; effects of, on practice, 122-123; organizations, 117-120; problems and trends of, 123; topics and findings, 120-123
Rui X., 49
Rural education. *See* Peasant education

S

Second Institute. *See* Shanghai Second Institute of Education
Second Revolutionary Civil War, and literacy education, 6
Self-study examinations: development of, 99-100; diplomas, certificates, and degrees for, 103-104; guidelines for, 104; for handicapped students, 60-61; institutions for, 104; methods of, 102-103; objectives of, 100; organizational structure of, 101; organizations for, 100-102; records management of, 103-104; in Shanghai, 104-106; testing for, 100
Shanghai: and institutional education, 67-73; peasant schools near, 25
Shanghai Adult Education Research Institute, 113, 120
Shanghai Adult Education Research Society, 119-120
Shanghai Artists Association, and handicapped, 62-63
Shanghai Association of the Blind and Deaf, 61-62
Shanghai Association of the Handicapped, 62-63
Shanghai Bulb Factory: and factory worker education, 38-39; and regular schools, 40-41; and worker education outside the factory, 40
Shanghai Education Bureau: and diplomas, 40; and worker examinations, 39
Shanghai Foreign Trade Worker University, as institutional school, 72-73

Shanghai High Pressure Oil Pump Plant: educational plan at, 42; importance of worker education at, 42-43; and worker education, 41-43

Shanghai Institute of Education, and special education, 61

Shanghai Municipal Education Bureau, and institutional education, 70-71

Shanghai Municipal Government: and adult educator training, 112; and educational support, 54

Shanghai Party Committee, and Shanghai Party School, 49

Shanghai Party School: and cadre education, 49-51; courses at, 49-50; examination at, 51; exchange activities at, 51; faculty of, 49, 50-51; major classes at, 50; selection for, 50

Shanghai Second Institute of Education, 110, 111-115; admission requirements for, 114; continuing education at, 114; future directions for, 115; and international relations, 114-115; programs of 113-114; staff and curriculum of, 112-113; students of, 113; vital statistics of, 112

Shanghai Second University of Industry (SSUI), 70

Shanghai TV University (STVU), 94-97; Chuansha Branch School of, 28-29; and curriculum, 96; disciplines at, 94-95; and institutional education, 73; instruction at, 95-96; and regular universities, 96; requirements for, 95; staff at, 94; students at, 95; success of, 97; training approaches at, 95-96; and worker education, 42

Shanghai Trade Union, and educational support, 54

Shanghai Worker Education Research Institute, and legislation, 122

Shanghai Worker's Cultural Palace, 54-58; art training at, 56-57; book reading and review at, 55; exhibitions at, 55; hobby activities at, 55-56; lectures at, 55; literature writing at, 56; performing artists and musicians at, 57; sports at, 57

Shenyang Association of Handicapped Youth, 63

Shenyang Kangfu Professional School, and special education, 63

Sixth Five-Year Economic Development Plan, 7; and literacy, 16

Social education, 8, 53-58; description of, 53-54; funds for, 53-54; and Shanghai Worker's Cultural Palace, 54-58; types of, 53

Somalia, 51

Soothill, W. E., 10, 11

Special education, 59-63; background of, 59-60. *See also* Handicapped people

Sports, as social education, 57

State Commission on Education, 10, 94, 120; and NACSSE, 100-102; and special education, 59-60, 61; and survey, 122

State Economy Committee, and examinations, 37

State Education Department, 30; and correspondence education, 76

State Higher Education Department, and university adult education, 75

State Statistics Bureau, and worker education, 33

Suggestions for Strengthening the Work of Cadre Education, 47

T

Teachers. *See* Adult educators

Ten Year Chaos, 7; and literacy, 16, 17; and university adult education, 76. *See also* Cultural Revolution

Third Plenary Session of the Eleventh Conference, 7, 23; and cadre education, 46-47, 48-49

Thirty-Ninth Amendment, and special education, 59

Trade Union of the People's Republic of China, and educational support, 54

Trade unions, and social education, 54

TV education. *See* Distance education

U

Unemployment, of handicapped people, 61-63

United States: and continuing education, 88-89; and professional exchange, 113, 114-115
University adult education, 75-81; and auditing, 81; background of, 75-76; and contractual training, 81. *See also* Correspondence education
University evening college, 79-80; period of study for, 80; teachers at, 80

V

Vocational education, for handicapped, 62-63

W

West Germany, 114
Worker education, 8, 33-43; content of, 34; degree programs in, 33-34; history of, 34; in large enterprises, 34-38; in medium-sized enterprises, 38-41; nondegree programs in, 33-34; in small enterprises, 41-43

Y

Yugoslavia, 51
Yunnan University, and handicapped student association, 60

Z

Zhang T., 5
Zhang W., 46
Zhongshan Institute, and special education, 61